MW00981013

STORY OF AN IMMIGRANT:

a Russian boy born in China prospers in Canada

by Alec Spiridonoff Noble

To my faithful wife and our two daughters who have been so tolerant in accepting my frequent absences over the period of my employment with Canadian Pacific.

FAMILY CHART

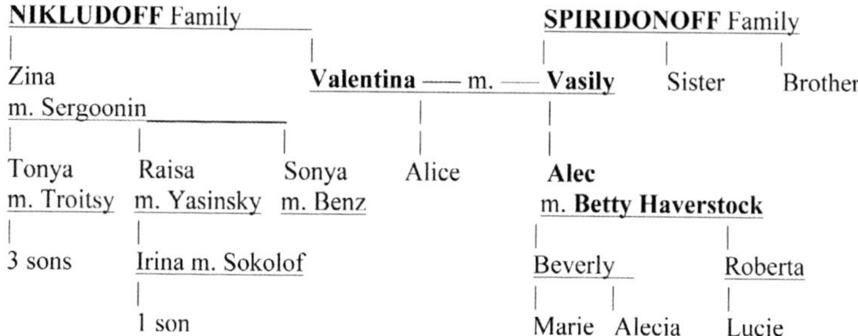

Genealogy

Over the years many of my friends have on numerous occasions posed the question, “Why don’t you write an account of your life and experiences? It would be a fascinating story.” Now that I have sat myself down with pencil and paper at hand, the mind is a blank as to where and how to start. Perhaps it would be appropriate to go back and account for my Russian background.

My father Vasili Platonavich Spiridonoff was from Siberia, born 19 January 1873 in an area adjacent to and registered in the City of Tomsk. He had one brother and a sister. The name Spiridonoff evidently originates with the Russian Orthodox Church where Icons of Saint Spiridonius were a popular item. My father received an education, however I have some reservations as to the extent since the only document I have as proof of the fact indicates that he graduated at the age of 10 years. The certificate in his name is from the City of Khabarovsk, thousands of kilometers east of his place of birth. This disparity is a mystery since subsequent contacts with his kin in later years were still made through Tomsk. One unique feature of the document in my possession is the statement that in view of the achieved scholastic standing he was to be exempt from military service.

My mother Valentina Nikludoff was born 6 December 1887 in Saratov in western Russia on the banks of the Volga River following an elder sister with the given name of Zina.

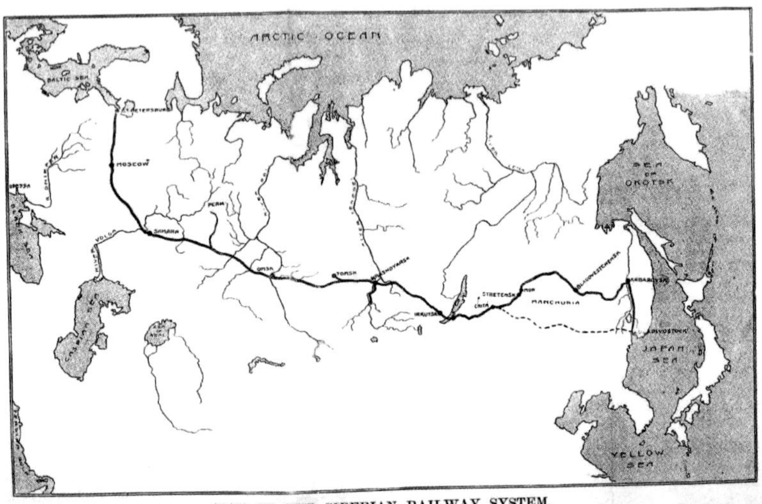

MAP OF THE SIBERIAN RAILWAY SYSTEM.

c. 1901 - Wikimedia Commons

Historical Elements

During the worldwide railway mania of 1850-60, Russia having absorbed Siberia into the Russian Empire, embarked on the possibility of a Trans-Siberian Railway to the Pacific. First proposals fell on deaf ears; however, in 1891 the government gave its official approval. The line was comparatively level and with the exception of a short distance in the area of Lake Baykal was fairly straightforward. Upon reaching Chita, the section of railway circumventing the Chinese province of Manchuria posed major problems.

With the coronation of Nicholas II in 1895, relations with China were much improved and the railway committee decided to approach the Chinese to allow a direct line to be built through the comparatively flat land of Manchuria. An agreement resulted to create the Chinese Eastern Railway stretching across Manchuria, permitting the completion of the Trans-Siberian Railway. The agreement went further and permitted the Russians to construct a branch line southward to Port Arthur.

My father was engaged starting from the construction phase on a 25-year contract and was first involved in the horse and wagon survey trek and was subsequently employed in the Harbin[1] division headquarters. There were many wild and aggressive tribes that looted construction camps and to keep

---

[1]See appendices starting on page 119 for further historical background.

order Russians became dominant in northern Manchuria. The line was complete and running from St. Petersburg (Leningrad) to Vladivostok in 1903-04.

Harbin, after the Russian Revolution of 1917, became a haven for refugees from Russia and for a time was the largest Russian city outside of the Soviet Union.

Manchurian Railway early 20th century. Wikimedia Commons

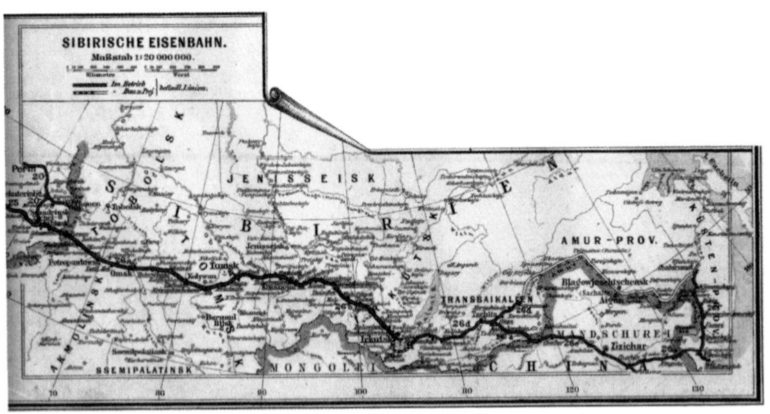

Historic map of the Trans Siberian Railroad. Harbin is located at the bottom between 120 and 130. Wikimedia Commons

China

Father arrived in Harbin sometime in 1901-1902. At the same time a Nicholas Nikludoff came on the scene as another railway employee. Whether he had a wife at the time or not I cannot verify. She could have passed away before his leaving Saratov or she may have expired shortly after this arrival due to plagues that were rampant in the primitive conditions. All that is known is that Nicholas was in China with two daughters, Zina and Valentina. Firstly, Zina married another railway worker with the surname of Sergoonin. Valentina shortl y thereafter married my father Vasili Platonovich Spiridonoff.

The first child in my immediate family was a daughter born 22 of December 1908, followed by my somewhat belated arrival on 21 September 1919.

We lived in a railway provided house, and across from us was the Sergoonin family. They had a spacious screened front porch and in the heat of the summer it was often used as a bedroom for the daughters Tanya, Raisa, and Sonja. Since they used to have the habit of sleeping late on the weekends when there was no school, it was my favorite prank in the early hours to go over there and, standing in the doorway, shout, "Sleepy heads, sleepy heads!" This would, of course, get them both agitated and aroused upon which I made a hasty retreat. While I was too young to attend a school, my sister and the other children of railway employees of school age were enrolled in institutions and were extended the opportunity for advanced education of university caliber all provided by the railway.

Winters were severe with a heavy snow and cold that provided outdoor skating with the ritual of hot roasted chestnuts for refreshment. One event that stands out in my memory is attending the funeral at a neighbor's house where their daughter was lying in a coffin in the living room having passed away as a result of a fall at the open air skating rink.

It was shortly afterwards that we moved to a newer home that provided, aside from our family quarters, room for native servants. The full detail of rooms and the layout I don't recall but I do remember that father always had a hand gun on the dresser in the bedroom. There was a small kitchen with another auxiliary one in the courtyard at the rear which was specifically for summer use. In the same walled-in yard there was a pit with a small wooden structure on the top fitted with a trap door into which we dumped all the waste and sewage from the house.

There was a rough dirt road in front of the house and an open field with a few scattered trees which my friends and I used to climb in the spring to feast on dried and very tasty petals following the spring bloom. Walks took us up over a small hill to the banks of the Sungari River where we used to sit and watch trains going over what seemed like a very long bridge.

In my estimation, life must have been very comfortable, as Sunday church was always followed by an elaborate luncheon with an evening of socializing and card games. It was much later that I learned what I was in fact seeing was a degree of stability achieved only after years of hardship and turmoil before my arrival on the scene. Shortly after my parents' arrival in China they evidently fortunately survived a cholera epidemic during which my father was seriously afflicted as a result of having partaken of some contaminated water. Limited available water led to dehydration and in the final analysis his survival is accredited to the fact that his intake of fluid was the consuming of brine from a barrel of dill pickles.

Following this cholera epidemic there was the Russo-Japanese war of 1904-05 when the Russian population was exposed to virtual annihilation and would have been had the conflict not been resolved by the Treaty of Portsmouth signed on August 29, 1905.

Summer was very hot and humid and we often spent free or vacation time out of the city on the other side of the Sungari River at an area of beautiful sand beaches surrounded by vacation cottages.

I recall on many occasions going shopping either just around the corner for small paper-wrapped sweets or with my parents to some of the major stores which were all operated by Russians. The only things we bought from the natives were fresh fruit and vegetables. These local merchants usually did their business from small sidewalk stands and the little sweet cantaloupe were the most tasty that I have ever eaten and will never forget. At these native markets it was very common to see women with their bound feet and most males with pigtails.

Russian domination of Manchuria was virtually in total. They brought in all the staff and established all the required services for the railway employees. The goods for the retail market were brought in from Russia, along with staff right down to the drivers to operate the horse drawn carriages for public transport. The Chinese were frozen out from every angle and benefited only by the placement of a few household servants or the sale of some fresh produce from the agricultural lands along the railway.

By the time Russia had gone through the revolution of 1917

and had come under Communist control with its socialism, the Manchuria community members were divided on the basis of their political leanings. Since many were under the 25-year contract, they were confronted with major decisions at the end of their employment. Those who approved of the changes pulled up stakes and returned to the place of their origin. Others opposed to Communism had grave misgivings about a regime which had assassinated the Tzar and were left at wits end. Should they stay in China and seek a method of survival or look for sanctuary somewhere else?

My father, not one who would subscribe to socialism or the Communist doctrine, elected to seek refuge in Canada. Fortunately at the time of the decision, the Canadian Pacific Railway was conducting a world-wide recruiting program in its endeavor to attract settlers for the Canadian prairie lands. Having completed the trans-continental railway they were extending cut-rate transportation as an incentive to prospective immigrants. Father was not alone in the choosing of Canada and many of his co-workers made the same decision. Others chose Brazil, Argentina, Australia or a host of other countries which took their fancy and offered a sanctuary. Considering what I now know, it is evident the choice was made only after deep thought and analysis; one that the family has been thankful for ever since. Applications were duly filed for the immigration and on their approval in late 1924 preparations were immediately commenced.

Father enrolled in a driving school that had a Model T Ford automobile, on some assumption that this would be a necessity in Canada. Mother went to a cooking school conducted by a very highly qualified and renowned French Chef, learning, of all things, the secrets of making many of the French pastries and candy. The effort on her part was a major success and the delicacies she produced in subsequent years will never grace a table again. Every ingredient had to be pure and meet a superior standard. Father's efforts at manipulating a motor vehicle were not quite as successful. He borrowed the driving school vehicle on graduation to take me on a demonstration drive only to manage an unscheduled stop with the trunk of a tree firmly implanted in the radiator. I do not recall seeing another automobile on the streets of Harbin in those days.

Departure day arrived with May 1925 and proved to be quite an event. Bags and trunks were assembled and what an array of goods we had. There were the prized possessions and clothing which was understandable, but some of the other goods belong in "Believe it or not." For example, there was a cast iron Hibachi, hammers, saws, folding cots, pots and pans, all on good advice and recommendations received from the migration promoters who were obviously very ignorant of circumstances at the intended destination.

We joined a group of some 25 families for our departure and boarded the railway south for Dairen as the first stage of our journey to the promised land. The entire Russian population must have gathered at the station to bid farewell.

My mind is a complete blank and I do not recall any of the events of the railway journey, the boarding of a ship or the sailing of the Yellow Sea to the Japanese port of Kobe, as I was not yet five years old. We stayed in Kobe for a week or ten days and I recall going to some very elaborate Japanese parks and gardens, as well as walking along streets looking at collapsed buildings and mountains of rubble that were the remains and evidence of the devastation of the earthquake of 1923. We were subsequently moved to Yokohama to board the Canadian Pacific liner Empress of Asia for our journey across the Pacific.

On the ship the entire immigrant group was housed in steerage and while meals were prepared by the vessel crew there was no dining room and members of our party were on a daily basis assigned chores such as the bringing of the prepared food to our quarters for consumption. One of the engine room crew evidently took a liking to me and I was fortunate in having him as an escort to all areas of the vessel, including the spending of many hours with him in the engine room. Again, I can't say how many days we were enroute and only the arrival at Vancouver on 25 June 1925 is lodged in my memory. On landing we were held in the immigration shed for processing down on the waterfront just west of the foot of present day Burrard Street.

The Bureau of Canadian Information 1920
CP Archives A.6199
Courtesy Canadian Pacific Railway Archives, Montréal, Quebec, Canada

My Life as a Canadian Begins

We were in due process all granted landed status and boarded a Canadian Pacific train in what were known as colonist cars to embark on another stage of our journey to the Promised Land. We arrived in Alberta at a point I have not been able to positively identify; it was either Ponoka or Rimbey or for that matter it could even have been Bluffton. We were transported by road to a centre established for the purpose of handling arriving immigrants administered by an agent of the railway, a Mr. Dournovo, who acted as an adviser to the incoming immigrants. There was a one-story building, which could be taken for a large hall within which each family staked out a territory for their sleeping area, and had use of a communal kitchen.

In our case we spent only a few nights in these cramped quarters and were fortunate to get possession of a small hut constructed by a previous immigrant, which consisted of one room dug out three-quarters of its height into the ground, approximately a two-foot wooden wall and a sod roof. To gain entry it was a case of going down several steps much like going into the basement of a modern house.

The immediate project facing all families of the group was the selection and purchase of land on which they were expecting to establish their future life and destiny. Some, having a look around, evidently appreciated the hardships to follow and immediately gave up the prospect of becoming farmers, packed their goods and despite previous agreements took off for greener pastures in the cities. Along with others, the Mishukoffs, Soboleffs, Troitskys, Osokins and Polushins, my parents elected to remain in the area, become farmers and be a party to free enterprise.

Each of the families eventually selected a site for their purchase and in our case we came into possession of a quarter section of land in a district known as Homeglen. This was bought from an earlier settler identified as Barney Farnum. I must point out that there was in fact little virgin land available at the time unless one was prepared to go into far removed territory away from the towns or rail services. Our choice was relatively civilized. After all, we were only 26 miles from Ponoka, 20 miles from Rimbey and 18 miles from the railway flag stop at Bluffton.

Canadian Pacific Rail, having sought settlers over the years, had introduced many as the railroad pushed westward and had in fact, early in the century, already sold much of the choice land to early arrivals. Many Americans that had ventured as pioneers into the mid-western states were very well prepared to part with their homesteads to the wealthy followers and in turn take advantage of CPR incentives to settle the Canadian prairie. Some, now in 1925, were well established farmers and remained but others who were to a degree on lands capable of only marginal production, grasped at the opportunity to sell at profits to the ignorant immigrants who had money to spend and knew zilch about land or the economics of farming.

A group of the newcomers, perhaps with a superior knowledge of agriculture, banded together and left the area for the Peace River country. Others remained and selected sites in the radius of some 40 miles from Rimbey to Westrose, Falun to Chesterwold, west through Homeglen, Springdale and other locations, names allocated to rural postal branches which served the farmers of the surrounding area. As stated, my father bought from Barney Farnum in the area identified as Homeglen. Others remained in the vicinity of some six to eight miles.

We moved to the farm during the course of August 1925 and embarked on a venture that was to prove disastrous in the following years. However, it must also be recognized that this was both the time and the place that my life as a Canadian began.

Father acquired some cows, chickens, pigs and turkeys for a start, all of which were supposed to reproduce and not only provide our basic food requirement but also generate a marketable surplus for revenue. During the course of the winter, at the expense of other venturesome farmers, we acquired some horses and farm implements when they were giving up their ambitions and, in our case, dreaming of the fortunes that were to come. We naturally had to be prepared for the agricultural aspect of the enterprise and the planting of cereal crops which were intended to be the bounty of the venture.

With the first of September I was enrolled in the Homeglen school, a common rural facility of one room, one teacher and some 20 students encompassing grades one to eight. If my memory serves me correctly, my first teacher was a Miss McQuarrie whom I had the pleasure of meeting at a reunion in the Homeglen Community Hall in July 1984. She was my first encounter with an introduction to not only school but also the English language. Inasmuch as going to school was supposed to be an adventure, it was even more than that for me. Here I was on the verge of six years of age with not one word of English at my command confronted with strange surroundings that had no relationship to my previous life with a governess. I guess it would be more appropriate to say that while the exposure was strange to me, it can only be taken as a sliver of the surroundings and circumstances that confronted my parents.

The little house had one room for general living and eating with a wood burning heater along the northern wall; a kitchen with a wood stove; one bedroom upstairs heated by the metal stove pipe that came from the living room below; one small unheated pantry off the kitchen; and one small room at the back of the house behind the living room which became the quarters for the hired hand. Water came from a well some 30 feet from the front door and the only other convenience was a two-holer some 90-100 feet behind the house.

Our immediate neighbor a half mile to the east on the north side of our road was Hans Neilsen, a further mile east on the south side of the thoroughfare was the Polushin family. One more farmer was some half a mile east of them and then there was vacant land for the next five miles before the next farm. Half a mile to the west was the Otto Jensen family of Danish origin, one of the Americans that was an immigrant from North Dakota. Another mile to the west was the Stewart family which had come from Scotland and made the raising of sheep their prime venture. Further on to the west were the Bates, the Moodys and then three Burns families. Of the Burns clan, their father had to be one of the earliest settlers in the region since the two brothers Bob and Roy were in fact second generation occupiers of the land. Roy left the farm for a period [during] the First World War. Along with other names that could be mentioned, despite the fact that we were spread over some six miles, these families all came under the classification of neighbors.

Shortly after getting established on the farm, my sister, now beyond the Homeglen school status, had little prospect ahead of her and in company with her friend and schoolmate from the orient, Clara Soboleff, left to seek employment in Edmonton. They both started as machine operators in the Great Western Garment factory (GWG) that is to this day one of the outstanding manufacturers of denim clothing. There was no fixed or guaranteed minimum wage and their earnings were based on piece work. She remained with that venture until 1932 when the depression confronted GWG with shrinking markets and confronted her with a layoff and she left to seek another occupation in Vancouver.

That first half of 1925 was a time we had no harvest to attend to and as a result it was an opportunity for Father to go into the Nanton and Vulcan regions south of Calgary to work on the more established and larger farms which had a need for assistance with their harvests.

My difficulties were the least of the first winter on the farm. The trials and tribulations for my parents in this new world must have been appalling after all the comforts of their lives in China. On Father's return from the harvesting he secured a job in a saw mill in the Hoadley area nearly 20 miles off to the northwest. After work on Saturdays he would walk home to spend Sunday cutting wood for our comfort and attend to other matters that were beyond Mother's ability. Then he walked back to his workplace on Sunday night.

While all I had to do was go to school during the week, Mother was going through the ordeal of looking after the acquired livestock, the likes of which she had previously only seen from a distance. Amazingly, all survived and we had an adequate supply of our own milk, butter and eggs. For other staples a neighbor in the normal farmer style of mutual assistance would make known the fact of a proposed journey into town and would in due course bring back the essentials of flour, salt, sugar and anything else required to satisfy the immediate needs.

It was during one of Father's absences that we had our first experience with a sick and mangy coyote which came down the road and decided to come right up to our door, obviously attracted by the smell of food. Mother was terrified and when the beast went around to the back of the house, she ran out the front door intending to get neighbor assistance. (Don't overlook that the nearest neighbor would be half a mile away.) Fortunately a stranger just happened to be passing and upon being hailed came to the rescue. He shot the animal and even went to the extent of taking the carcass away for disposal.

The one room Homeglen school served all the children for a radius of two miles in each direction. It had one teacher, an average enrollment of about 25 and covered grades one to eight. I started grade one on September 25 with not one word of English at my command and recall one instance on walking to school having Rodney Jensen pointing to a rise in the land saying "big hill." While there were others in my category lacking linguistic ability, it is surprising how soon we acquired a capability through the total immersion and involvement in all the school activities. The walks to and from school were the hardest part as winter brought with it heavy snow, a lot of wind with temperatures that at times dipped into the minus 30 F. range.

With the arrival of spring, having now acquired some horses and implements with the fall and winter earnings, came the cultivation of the land for our first planting of wheat, oats and barley. There also had to be a garden concentrated on vegetable varieties which could be stored for winter consumption, potatoes, turnips, carrots and beets, as well as cabbage that could be made into sauerkraut, plus peas and beans for fresh eating and canning. Corn, cukes, tomatoes and fruit were out of the question as the summers were too short to mature the varieties available at the time.

Summer was the time to clear and break land to expand the cultivated area as well as the cutting and stacking of hay for the winter livestock feed. Our roads were strictly dirt turning to a quagmire with the spring thaw. Likewise after every rain, travel was restricted to horseback for days because of the famous prairie gumbo texture.

In 1927, Rodney Jensen having finished his grade eight started a weekly service with a team of horses and a democrat into Ponoka. He left at daybreak for the 52 mile round trip arriving home late at night and, if the roads were not at their best, often not until the next day. This was a welcome service as it now provided a method of weekly marketing of butter and eggs and the first revenue of our efforts. We had no refrigeration which required our milk to be put through a separator with the cream converted into butter and the skim milk given either to calves or the pigs. To keep the butter and other perishable food we used to put everything into a container and hang it down to the water level in the well.

Rodney maintained the service for about a year until it was replaced by a truck operated by the Ponoka Creamery driven by a deaf Mr. Crawford. He came through the district twice a week in the summer and once a week in winter. His service also provided for the delivery of anything from provisions to machinery parts on request and payment for these would be deducted from the monthly creamery cheque. The schedule was on a rain or shine basis and while residents knew enough to stay off the soft roads, he would come through regardless of conditions, thereby leaving six ruts in the road. These required the use of horse drawn road scrapers operated by farmers on the route, with compensation being deducted from their taxes.

Municipal authorities levied minimal taxes, however, since money was scarce only the better established farmers were in a position to pay. As mentioned above, others were given the option of doing road maintenance work including the repairing of bridges or just cutting brush keeping road allowances from being overgrown or the clearing of new right of way.

Socializing was a winter activity concentrated on events at the school. A Christmas concert was put on by the children, with any costume requirements made of paper. The teacher provided the music on a pump organ, after which Mr. Stewart would play Santa Claus with a present for each child of the community. Then there would be three or four dance nights with music by Rodney on his accordion and Ernest Moody with a violin. These events were promoted to raise money for the Christmas presents and the summer picnic prizes. The methods were unique box or shadow socials and sometimes Whist games for penny anti jackpots.

The box social had ladies prepare a hamper of evening refreshments, decorated and made most attractive. These would be put up on an auction basis and the buyer would be required to spend the refreshment hour with the supplier. In the case of shadow socials, ladies posed behind a white bed sheet with a background bright light and the image displayed was again auctioned with the successful bidder having to spend the supper hour with his purchase. Attendance at those events would be by horse and sleigh and invariably a couple of the conveyances would be the repository of a jug or two of moonshine.

Our third winter was brightened by the purchase of a battery operated radio. Unlike what we see today, it was a box affair three feet wide, two feet high and the same in depth, manufactured by the King Corporation with a 20-inch diameter Atwater Kent speaker sitting on top. On the floor was an array of batteries with one wet (of the car type) plus two sets of dry cells, six each type “A” and “B”. This all required an outside antenna of 100 feet of copper wire strung between the tops of two tallest trees. While it was sparingly used to conserve the power supply, we could nevertheless now have both music and news from the radio stations of both Calgary and Edmonton. Reception improved with the colder, clear nights and we could even hear the broadcasts from Spokane. The contraption was most welcome as the only music previously heard in the home was on a neighbor’s

Edison gramophone with its limited supply of cylindrical type records.

Other than that, we youngsters spent winters frolicking in the snow and I must say enjoyed the cold crisp days when out of school. There was always some skating in the local muskeg or along a creek, evenings of sleigh riding down what Rodney Jensen had called the big hill, where in fact our downhill glide was only a matter of 50 meters. What I probably enjoyed most was to ski on the banks and ditches on the side of the roads. A partner would get on a horse, gallop down the road and at the end of some hundred feet of rope would be me on skis riding over the humps and bumps on a wild terror of a ride.

Only one event was staged in the summer, being a community picnic at the end of June and the school year. Then we had baseball, horseshoe throwing and the children in all forms of races, the three-legged, the wheelbarrow plus the jumping and running. For this gathering, each family contributed food of their preparation with tables usually laden to the breaking point. For these picnics we always had Otto Jensen operate a refreshment stand with pink lemonade, candy and other small favors, but no ice cream.

There was little visiting between farmers except for an occasional game of chess or cards. The Russian settlers, despite distances, maintained contact traveling by horse drawn conveyances. The Soboleffs from Falun usually came on an overnight basis. We did the same if we were to visit the Mishukoffs at Rimbey.

In our district the occupied lands were fenced and all the vacant area was open range. As a result, after the morning milking the cattle were put out the gate to forage where they chose during the day. It was one of my daily duties after school to seek them out and herd them back for the evening milking. On completion of my first year of school, having acquired a puppy of mixed and doubtful breeding, he became a faithful servant and constant companion for my herding for all the years on the farm. It became a very common practice to go out, find the herd, give him the order to go home and have him take them right to the barn door while I detoured either to visit the neighbors or go back to school for a game of ball. When we were about to leave the farm, he went to live with the Mishukoffs and served them faithfully for the rest of his days.

The coming of fall 1926 brought our first harvest. The grain was cut with a binder and horses and had to be stacked for drying in preparation for the threshing which was again a communal activity on a mutual assistance basis. Bob Burns owned a McCormick Deering tractor, while his brother Roy owned the threshing machine. In the company of some eight or ten farmers with their teams and wagons, they would start at one end of the community working from farm to farm to complete the gathering of the year's bountiful harvest. On each farm two or three of the nearest wives would come to help the lady of the house in preparing both the lunch and dinner to feed the entire crew, as this was the responsibility of the host.

In this process all the harvesting was accomplished for all participants with the only money changing hands being to the Burns brothers for their machinery. If they so chose, they were entitled to a small percentage of the grain to market along with their own.

That first crop produced a good yield of No. 2 Northern Wheat which was wagon delivered to the Pool elevator in Ponoka for respectable prices, with the oats and barley being retained for livestock feed. The following year 1927 produced another good harvest and we, as a result, acquired a second quarter section followed by a third in 1928. Our efforts were rewarding to the point where we acquired a tractor and heavier machinery, planted greater acreage and truly considered our surroundings as the land of opportunity and plenty. With the added cultivation we now engaged a hired hand to help with the haying and harvesting. We provided room and board plus a wage of one dollar per day worked, which often meant as much as fourteen hours.

In the winter we used to enjoy a change from our normal diet by having fresh frozen whitefish supplied by Native Indians. These hardy people from the reservation at Hobema, in the dead of winter, as a group of some four or five families with sleighs and horses, would trek across the country making overnight stops by the roadside, pitching their teepees for their shelter enroute to Battle or Buck Lakes to go ice fishing. After spending a couple of weeks and filling their carrying capacity, they would start the return journey, stopping at farms and trading fish for the likes of eggs, flour, potatoes or any other items of which they were in need. These same people used to make a similar trek during the summer months in their gathering of blueberries in the pine forests to the north of our farm. They repeated the procedure selling their product in exchange for the produce of the farms they passed on the return to the reservation.

Other than for food, 90 percent of our shopping was either through the Eaton's or Simpson's catalogue. Consequently we were very dependent on the postal services in more ways than one. The first couple of years the facility was operated by the Bates family from their home. Following this it was taken over by Mr. and Mrs. Ridiough. He had a small Ford truck and made a trip into Bluffton once a week carrying both outgoing and incoming mail. It was a service still in effect at the time of our departure. If one made the three-mile trip to get mail, it was a common courtesy to pick up for anyone else along the way and drop it off on passing. Our nearest telephone was at the Stewart farm, which was the end of the line that came from Rimbey and was not extended to reach our place during our tenure.

By the time I was ten years of age [1929], I was proficient with a 22 rifle and not only supplemented our table with partridge and prairie chicken but earned some money as well. Rabbits were a virtual plague and at one time there was a good market for the white pelts during the winter. Father and I would shoot them by the dozen a day, spending the evenings skinning and stretching the pelts on specially designed boards for drying. These brought as much as 13 cents each from the fur buyers. There was a rare weasel or squirrel that could be sold for up to two dollars and I made it a practice of setting a string of traps along a creek all winter long, checking them morning and night on my way to and from school. In the summer there was another opportunity for earnings by robbing crow and magpie nests of their eggs or catching gophers, all of which were sold for two cents each.

I finally reached financial self-sufficiency at the age of 12 and was no longer dependent on crows or gophers when I became employed as the school janitor with a monthly salary of two dollars and fifty cents. This meant that after school each day I had to sweep the floor and clean the blackboards. When it started to cool in the fall, I had to be at the school one hour before anyone else, start the wood stove and have the place warmed for others on their arrival. In the depth of winter, it meant attending the stove during the day as well. After school I not only had to sweep and clean but also had to bring in enough wood for the following day. With this responsibility on my hands I acquired a pony to ride, keeping it in the little stable at the school during the day.

We were stricken with disaster in 1929. The first was the loss of a large proportion of the turkey flock. These birds, while they roosted in the trees around the house and barn at night, were notorious wanderers in the undeveloped bush country, going as much as a mile from home during the day. One evening instead of our 70 to 75 birds, only a dozen or so showed up. The next day a search located them all, victims of a raid by coyotes. There went the income they could have generated at their sale for the Christmas season and the few rare luxuries that it could have provided. But, worse was yet to come. The grain fields started to wither and die. There was not a drop of rain throughout the growing season, and when harvesting came we managed to salvage little more than the seed that had been put in the ground in the spring. This was an incalculable loss and to survive the winter meant the premature sale of some of the cattle and pigs.

To conserve on money we relied more than ever on our own resources and as an example of the assistance of a neighbor and his truck we took a load of wheat to the Brackman Kerr mill in Wetaskiwin to have it processed. They operated a facility that was made available to the farmers wherein they kept a percentage of wheat brought in as a charge for the services and returned the balance not only as flour but all the other components that resulted, such as the bran and cream of wheat cereal.

The following year was marginally better. We had rain and the crops grew but before the summer was over we lost a large proportion to hail and from then on things only got worse with the onset of the depression. Prices tumbled to the point that all our efforts produced hardly enough to meet expenses. By the fall of 1932 the hired man was gone and I became his replacement at the ripe age of 13. When school started in September there was no question of going back to school until the harvest was in and as a result I spent the month on the tractor with Father on the combine behind or looking after the handling of the grain. The year ended without our meeting expenses which resulted in another premature sale of some livestock, only this time it was not as easy as the previous year.

We hired a farmer with his truck, loaded it up with a dozen prize steers and drove to the Burns slaughter house in Edmonton looking forward to some ready cash. On our arrival the buyer came over to the truck, looked over the stock and selected a grand total of seven animals as acceptable. They had such a surplus of cattle that the market was very limited and we ended up driving home with five still on board, with only a fraction of the expected monetary return.

Our final effort for success came with 1933 in the spring planting season. I was again kept out of school running the tractor during the day, with Father coming out at supper time to take over and run the machine during the night. Despite missing a period of a couple of weeks in the spring and again during the harvest season, I still made respectable marks and was handed a certificate for completing grade eight. As for quantity, our fields were of a medium category, but the hand writing was on the wall when the prices being paid were considered. Before the harvest was even started, the decision had been made to cease further effort.

Immediately after the harvest, the farm was put up for sale and a deal was concluded about the first of October to another farmer who was moving north from his previously failed enterprise of growing sugar beets in the Brooks region southeast of Calgary. I am not certain but it seems that we got something like a thousand dollars and he assumed the due payments. Our best wheat in that year brought 18 cents a bushel on being delivered to the elevator and our eggs were bringing in only four cents a dozen.

An auction sale was scheduled for 30 October 1933 and upon its conclusion we were through, leaving only with the clothes on our backs and a few prized possessions which we had carried from the orient, a few callouses and a lot of memories. The goal now was to join my sister in Vancouver where she was already established in a rented apartment. In Rimbey we made a deal with one of the migrant workers who had a car and wanted to go to Vancouver. It was agreed that he supply the vehicle and we would pay expenses.

That started us on our way and the arrangement had the lengthy duration of one day. Before we got through Red Deer our driver got into an accident and the car was immobilized. We parted company and took the train to Calgary, stopping there for a few days with former Homeglen residents to make arrangements for the onward journey.

Again after some inquiries we found a couple with a new car who were setting off on a move to the coast and on a basis similar to the previous one we set off once again. At the time there was no passable auto road through the mountains and our route was therefore to take us to the U.S. border at the Kingsgate border crossing, then over U.S. highways to Seattle and [north to] Vancouver. Misfortune dogged us again upon arriving at the border. As we had not yet become Canadian citizens we were refused entry by the authorities, forcing us to abandon the second attempt at an automobile trip. At that point we boarded a train and proceeded to the west.

Our failure as entrepreneurs and tillers of the soil was not the result of a lack of effort but circumstances. Firstly, we were a party to the second wave of settlers buying land with the obligation of payments and interest. Secondly, the elements of nature, hail or drought, and thirdly, the depression and its market prices. Many survived the obstacles, however, they were the original settlers that had acquired their lands as homesteaders or token payment and had no financial burden. Others had families of able bodied souls that could venture afield, seeing earnings and provide the means of survival. Father was now 60 and I a mere 14.

Railway Travel in Canada 1929
CP Archives A.16185
Courtesy Canadian Pacific Railway Archives,
Montréal, Quebec, Canada

Vancouver

On arrival in Vancouver via the C.P. Kettle Valley rail line sometime in the middle of November, we moved into an apartment with my sister (Suite 5-2215 West First Ave.), rent 10 dollars per month. She was working as a sales clerk for the Hudson's Bay Company and while the wages were not that great, it provided a regular weekly pay cheque. The surroundings were strange for me, being hemmed in on all sides by houses and apartment blocks. People that were neighbors by proximity. not actually knowing one another, going about their interests without so much as a hello and totally lacking the spirit of the farm community.

One of the first experiences in the big city was a venture downtown on a walking tour with my father. Burrard Street Bridge had been opened only the previous year and we walked over it noting the Granville Street on our right, planning to return over it. We walked [through] city centre and in due course came to a bridge that we crossed, unbeknown to us that we were now headed south over the Cambie Street Bridge which was identical to the Granville with its centre swing span. The landmarks we had noted were not to be found and after roaming around to the point of exhaustion finally had a taxi take us home. That was not my only experience of getting lost, as it also happened on the first couple of days when I had trouble finding my way home after enrollment at Kitsilano High School at 10th Avenue and Larch Street.

My first objective was to enroll for school and on presenting myself with the grade eight graduation certificate from Homeglen, I was readily accepted and placed into grade nine with a prescribed list of subjects. (English, Social Studies, Math, French, Music and the industrial arts – metal and wood working.)

From that first day my troubles started and multiplied. In the first case, it was the matter of having a different teacher for each subject and the fact that each class was in a different room. Having come from a one room, one teacher environment, my first downfall came after the first period when I was overwhelmed by the mass of students going in all directions in the hallways. I had no idea of the meaning behind all the shuffling, and when bells sounded, I was back in the same room that I was in for the first period of the day. Here I sat through another period on the same subject that I had already heard, with one exception in that all around me were strange new faces. As soon as that was over, I reported to the Principal's office to declare that my class was lost and I didn't know where they had gone.

In short order it was established that I was now supposed to be in French class and was duly escorted to the proper room. Here came the next problem in that the Vancouver schools started French in Junior High and here I was in third year French, never having even heard that there was such a language. The same disoricntation was to plague me, as both of the industrial arts courses were not only in different rooms but also in separate buildings. Somehow I found my way to Electrical where everyone was wiring up boards with bells and buttons with a few lights in between and all I could do was stand and stare. Having never experienced electricity prior to arrival in Vancouver and having had no instructions in such in Homeglen, it was mind boggling. It even went further than that when it came to Algebra and Geometry, as a rcsult of which by the end of the school year I was a total failure and scheduled to repeat grade nine the following year.

In the meantime Father was looking for work with little success. He delivered flyers for a printing house that went bankrupt and never got paid. With a friend (another destitute farmer) they started a sharpening of lawn mowers, a venture that went nowhere. Mother took advantage of her training in French cookery and started to make some of her specialties under an arrangement with a small store at Cornwall and Yew Streets that did the display and marketing. It again was just the wrong time for fancy baked goods when people could ill afford them when their prime concern was for butter, bread, milk, eggs and meat.

There was a better return from another venture that my sister promoted with the Hudson's Bay in getting their agreement to market a small waist, multi-patterned apron. We bought a new Singer electric sewing machine, bolts of cloth of various patterns from Wabasso Cottons and started a production line in the apartment. Father did the cutting, Mother the sewing, and in the evenings I would, after homework, sit at the machine while Mother ironed the finished goods and sister did the folding and packaging into dozen lots.

Our first order was for a gross and with their acceptance in the market place, further orders followed to keep us busy providing reasonable finances for a couple of years. This cottage industry was eventually forced out of business by the intrusion of major manufacturers and their assembly line production.

With me at school by the second year, I had acquired a bicycle and got myself a weekend job working for a Chinese green produce merchant on 4th Ave. at Yew Street. That venture was one to stay with me for years to come. Aside from making the odd delivery, the prime work was washing and trimming celery, and when each weekend was over I was permeated with the smell of celery to the point of an aversion to the product for many years. Another task that I will never forget was at Christmas time when they sold boxes of Japanese Mandarin oranges that at the time had a price tag of some 75 cents per box. In the back of the store we used to open every box, dump them out and repack the contents in a loose fashion, having at least six oranges left over that were then destined for over the counter sales by the dozen.

There were brighter horizons on my mind and with the view of securing a monthly income (much the same as the school janitor), I went in search of a paper route that could be handled after school. These too were not easy to acquire as many capable students were after the same thing. My first route was along Pender St. from Richards to Carral, the next one was Granville St. from Robson to Pacific, the third on Hornby St. again from Robson to Pacific. These regions, while downtown as it is known today, were residential, either people in hotel-apartment units or in fact in private houses. We worked out of a paper shack off Richards and Robson which involved riding my bike all the way into town after school until the time that I finally got a route covering Fifth and Sixth avenues between McDonald and Blenheim streets.

These routes were for the period of school days, and for the summer vacation I established a contact with a Mr. Trunkfield of the London Grocery Stores and became a delivery boy for the months of July and August, firstly for their store at 5th Ave. and Victoria Dr. and then at Main and Eighth Ave., subsequently ending up the next year at 70th Ave. and Cartier St. in Marpole.

In the meantime Father secured employment through a friend at Jones Tent and Awning at 43 West Hastings Street to work as an assistant to their accountant Mr. Smart. Here he played a dual role in that his duties of compiling the payroll related to the piece workers in manufacturing was supposed to take up the hours from 6 p.m. to midnight, after which he was provided accommodation to spend the night and in effect act as a watchman until 7 a.m. Now with sister working, Father with a job and me with a paper route, things started to look up.

My attendance at school for a second attempt at grade nine resulted in a passing to grade ten, but despite my best efforts, in June 1936 the year was assessed incomplete and some subjects would have to be repeated. I took exception to the failures that were on my report and had a confrontation with my homeroom teacher, a Mr. Haverstock. A lengthy discussion ended up with the implication that my efforts and progress were not of the desired standard and that it would be of mutual benefit for both the school and me if I would leave and not come back. The episode incensed me to the point of a decision to get even with him someday, not imagining as to how or when.

Considering the nature of my departure from school, my mind was made up that I was not about to go back and on announcing the decision at home it resulted in a dialogue that is better not recorded here. The next objective was to find employment, determined that I was quite capable of making it on my own through effort rather than spend any more time in an institution that was not to my liking.

Vancouver was a different city in those days. The west end was houses rather than apartments, even the downtown streets of Hornby, Howe, Seymour, Richards, Homer and Hamilton were houses from one end to the other. While the east side and Mount Pleasant were well developed, settlements were concentrated in Kitsilano, Point Grey or Marpole, leaving extensive unoccupied areas in between. Movie theatres were the prime sources of entertainment spread throughout the neighborhoods and we attended them on a regular basis to see double features with cartoons and news reels all for the general admission of 10 to 25 cents. As for the business district there were only 16 multi-story office buildings, the most prestigious of which was the Marine Building at 355 Burrard Street and six major hotels.

Canada • Provinces, Territories, Capitals - ThinkStock

Early Employment

In May 1936 my sister suffered a nervous breakdown and became a patient of the Vancouver General Hospital. The prognosis was poor and in due course she was relegated to the mental institution at Essondale. Despite the due efforts, her mental capacity deteriorated. There she was to remain for the rest of her days. The loss of her earnings was not to be taken lightly and I now felt an obligation to step in and fill the gap, having already made up my mind that school was not for me.

On the 24th of June, immediately on getting out of school, I made my first and only venture as a seeker of employment, going by streetcar to the corner of Granville and Hastings streets not knowing where I was headed or what I was looking for other than the fact that it had to be a paying job. Standing there looking around, I caught sight of a large sign at the foot of Granville reading "Canadian Pacific Spans the World." Recognition of the name stirred me into action and a mad charge into the employment office in the station.

With some assistance from a very official Tommy Barnard, an application was finally completed and along with an interview consuming some hour and a half, the formalities were completed. To me that was enough of an ordeal for one day and having no idea of where else to go called it a day, went home and down to the beach. Little did I know of the consequences that were to follow.

Shortly after having joined my friends on the beach for a ballgame, it was a surprise to see my mother coming across the park on a search and on meeting handed me a telephone number to call as soon as possible. On placing the call I discovered it was none other than Tommy Barnard that I had seen in the morning and our conversation was short and to the point.

"Do you have a bicycle?"

"Yes."

"Want to start work tomorrow morning?"

"Yes."

"O.K. Bring your bike and report to Wally Taylor at the Telegraph Office at 428 West Hastings St. at nine o'clock."

That was it, my fate was sealed, and the following day I was outfitted with a uniform and started delivering telegrams on a commission basis. Here was the beginning of my association with the Canadian Pacific organization for the next 46 and a half years until my election to take an early retirement on the 31st of December 1982.

There was no minimum or fixed wage and our income as messengers was strictly based on the number of telegrams handled for which we were paid on a sliding scale. This depended on distance ranging from three cents each for the immediate central area, rising to a maximum of $1.00 if we were required to make a delivery into Burnaby or Richmond as far as Steveston. The average monthly earning was usually around $30.00, including the occasional tip. When the winter weather with its fog, rain or snow made cycling both trying and hazardous many were the temptations to seek another venture.

We were on occasion assigned to courier services carrying

freight billings between railway offices or the news reports from Canadian Press to the local newspaper offices, in which event we were paid 25 cents per hour. There were about 20 of us and most worked during the regular day. We rotated and had to take our turn at evenings, weekend, holidays or the graveyard shift. It soon became evident to me that the staff in the office were former messengers.

During the course of the next three years I saw many changes in our group, as co-workers would transfer to become telegraph operators, go to the Drake Street shops or depart on other ventures. My sights were set to follow those that remained with the company and as my seniority increased so did my effort at perfection to stay in the limelight for possible consideration and promotion.

In the summer of 1938 I received my first entitlement for a vacation of two weeks and as an employee acquired the concession of a free rail pass. There loomed the opportunity and there could be no alternative more satisfying than to go right back to Alberta and renew my carefree days of childhood on the farm. With a rail pass in hand I checked my bicycle as baggage and departed for Calgary, riding coach on a wicker seat and a bag of sandwiches to keep me for the journey. At Calgary I changed to the Calgary-Edmonton line northbound for Lacombe, there to continue my trek by bike. The fact that it was some 30 miles to Rimbey didn't worry me in the least and I duly set off for the Mishukoff farm. Being mid-summer, riding by the fields and wide open spaces was exhilarating and I arrived at their place to be welcomed with open arms.

After a couple of days I proceeded on to Homeglen to visit with our former neighbors, the Jensens, Burns, Neilsens and Polushins. The very sight of all the familiar locations brought back memories of the days of rabbits, crows, magpies, the partridge grouse and gophers that were all such a big part of my childhood. Helping with the farming chores and riding the tractor were second nature. The aroma of fresh cut hay was better than any scent that can be manufactured.

After that sojourn I returned to my employment and immediately enrolled in the Pitman Business College for a night course in accounting, shorthand and typing. After all, my father was an accountant and railroader. What better vocation could I choose despite the trials and tribulations of his experience? Other fields could be worse.

I continued my effort and application to the job and was duly called upon to replace a Wharf Freight messenger taking his two week vacation. That was an introduction to a fixed salary and involved taking waybills for all arriving grain cars as they advance to elevators on the waterfront, on the return picking up the scale tickets for the cars that had been unloaded. My immediate superior was an Evelyn McNaughton and we got along famously. I left the office in the morning calling at each elevator to the Pool at Second Narrows, coming back with the tickets, repeating the tour in the afternoons.

During the visit of King George VI and the Queen to Vancouver in 1939, I was assigned as media messenger stationed at the Hotel Vancouver to carry all press releases to the telegraph office. It seems strange to look back on those days when I, a mere messenger, went in and out through all the security without anyone so much as blinking an eye.

Shortly after that assignment I was called into the office of a Mr. Bellis who informed me they were all very pleased with my efforts and he was willing to consider a transfer to other permanent employment. He was very frank about the problems with a name like Spiridonoff and suggested that I consider a change to something more in common acceptance. He was, in such an event, prepared to extend every consideration and as far as I was concerned, if it were necessary, it would be done.

I visited a lawyer in the Rogers building and by virtue of a document called a Deed Poll became Alec Noble with no more effort than the stroke of a pen. Registering this fact with Canadian Pacific pleased Mr. Bellis, who extended the assurance of a placement somewhere within the company.

To my surprise this did not take long and when Roy Bertram left the Wharf Freight office, I replaced him as the document carrier on the grain elevator services while I was still on the messenger pay scale. It was now a fixed rate of 30 cents an hour without the piece work scramble. The two daily trips and one on Saturdays were relatively leisurely, no more of the shifts, weekends or holidays.

In late 1939 we were to learn that my sister's state was deteriorating and the prognosis was very bleak. The treatments had no appreciable success and we were advised not to look forward of any possibility of her return to a normal life. There will be no way of explaining the reflection of this disaster on my parents or the determination on my part to make every contribution within my power to at least give them the satisfaction of being successful in my endeavors.

At this time in 1939 we bought a house at 2906 West 5th Ave. and having a tenant on the premises remained for the time being in our suite. Little did we know that war was to come or the housing restrictions that were to apply. While we had the intention of moving in when the current lease expired, we found ourselves precluded from forcing an eviction. The laws of the time prevented such an action and as a result we remained in the apartment until 1947 when we could get possession of a property that we owned.

On the 8th of April 1940 to my surprise I was summoned to the employment office by Tommy Barnard for an interview and duly informed that I was being transferred out of Wharf Freight. As he related the circumstances, I had to restrain myself from jumping with joy. The job, junior clerk in the

Purchasing Department in the station starting the next day with a salary of $60 per month, was nearly double my capacity as a bicycle courier. The rest of the day was spent getting a suit, white shirts, a tie and new shoes, with all being pressed, brushed and polished.

The next day found me at the office door, room 412 in the station, before starting time and once the introductions were over, I was directed to my own office desk with a list of my duties in hand – attend to both the in and out mail, file requisitions and invoices, and since there were no copy machines in those days, type copies as required, and run errands. I was in my glory now on regular office hours, five and a half days per week, clean and pleasant surroundings among very cooperative co-workers.

With World War II having been declared the previous September, it was a time when many of my friends were enlisting in the services. I considered the same, however, having just been placed into the Purchasing Department, the prime concern at the time was the job itself and insuring establishment with employment and wages. As a result I enlisted in the Royal Canadian Engineer Reserve, getting some training two evenings per week and spending my two-week vacation time at a military camp, William Head outside Victoria, in 1940 and at Nanaimo in 1941.

In the office I soon learned that purchasing was a complex and varied business, with the railway part only a portion of the enterprise. Our office served all the requirements of Canadian Pacific Rail, Canadian Pacific Steamships, B.C. Coast ships, the hotels, the golf courses, the Canadian Australasian Line, the Union Steamship Co. of New Zealand, the interior lake steamers and any other enterprise in which Canadian Pacific had an interest. The office had two people buying the hardware range, two people on commissary, one on stationery, two on lumber ties and timber, plus another five staff to look after the paperwork.

My attending the Pitman College was rewarded on completing my first year in the office and I became a junior steno clerk with a raise to $75 per month. The duties changed to helping various buyers as required, typing some of their correspondence and helping with the telephone placing of orders, while my junior position was filled with a new employee Norman Hogg.

Arrival of deep sea ships was a hectic time as a result of their short stay in port. Once at the dock, we would receive three requisitions, one each from the Chief Officer, the Chief Steward and the Chief Engineer listing all their requirements for the next voyage. The lists were varied and there was always the deadline of scheduled departure. Everything had to be delivered and every invoice signed as to receipt by the respective officer. That was one of my tasks and many were the times that I got off the ship just as the gangplank was about to be removed. The food orders were massive as by the time I got involved with helping on the commissary desk the majority of vessels coming into port were engaged in troop carrying and provisioned accordingly. Some came to pick up the likes of the Seaforth Highlanders that were destined for Hong Kong, while others brought in trainee airmen from Australia and New Zealand to attend the Commonwealth Air Training schools in Canada.

The worst experience of my life came late in 1941 when the M.S. Awatea arrived from the South Pacific with a compliment of airmen and was being supplied for an intended voyage requiring the catering for 3,000 men for a period of 60 days. Their order for food was something to behold -- flour by the ton, sugar the same, beef something like a hundred sides, everything imaginable down to the likes of 100 pounds of pepper. Few were the items that were in themselves less than a truck load.

I was assigned to help with the phoning and placing of the orders, handed a requisition for the frozen items of both fruit and vegetables covering every article from A to Z specifying 24 c/s of each. In my usual diligence to perform, I contacted every cold storage house in the city, placing the orders for what they had available going to the extent of calling Mission, Chilliwack and Abbotsford to fill the deficiencies. By four-thirty in the afternoon, truckloads of frozen goods were arriving at the ship side and at two minutes before quitting time, I got a phone call from the Chief Steward wanting to know what was going on. We had a relatively heated conversation only to establish that he being an Australian used the term c/s to mean cups rather than cases. Since the articles came 24 cups to the case, he actually wanted one case of each for the Captain's table and as the trucks went by, he removed one case to meet his requirement, sending the balance on their way as not required. This was a disaster of major proportions. What do you do with a fleet of trucks with perishable goods when the business day had already concluded? The mad scramble began to find storage space before a thaw rendered the items useless. I called every resource that I knew and even resorted to the police to find contacts. To my salvation, everything was in an appropriate storage about ten o'clock that night.

The next day, with the ship gone, the facts became known in the office and to my dismay, it was all treated very lightly and the incident faded as just another hazard of the occupation.

It was now late 1941 and events were indicating that the war effort was becoming far more demanding. Canada was on the verge of introducing conscription to fill the military demand and my thoughts turned to volunteering into a selected service rather than await the draft. To a degree the vision of my recent experience with a troop ship was prominent in my mind and fearing another incident that could jeopardize my occupation, I decided to enlist in the Air Force. My application was accepted and on taking a leave of absence effective 01 December 1941, I was off to fight the war.

Since I have in the previous chapter mentioned recreation while on the farm, it might be appropriate to mention our recreation in the 1937-1941 era. The summer days were primarily for the beach and the park with the tennis courts. When I had achieved a salary status with money in my pocket, it was very common to go for evening roller skating at the numerous rinks in town or go dancing at the Alma Academy at Broadway and Alona, the Embassay on Davie, the Alecandra on Robson or Happyland on the PNE grounds. There were, of course, the movies where we saw double features for a matter of a quarter and to the more athletic the bowling alleys where a five pin game cost 10 cents.

CPR Logo 1929 - 1946-
CP Archives CPRL6
Courtesy Canadian Pacific Railway Archives,
Montréal, Quebec, Canada

Young Alec in his Canadian Pacific messenger uniform.
Beverly Belanger collection

The War Years

Having seen and read many movies and books relative to World War II, my participation having been minimal, justifies only a short account of my experiences in uniform.

Given a transportation warrant I was sent to Mo. 3 Manning Depot at Edmonton to be uniformed and go into basic training. It was only a matter of three weeks before I was granted a week of leave and, with a rail pass in my pocket, took the first available train to Vancouver. (Enlisting in the services did not forfeit any of the privileges due to one from his employer.) It must have been quite a surprise to everyone both at home and the office to see me on furlough after less than a month of service. They had all given me quite a sendoff to fight a war and here I was home on leave just three weeks after the fond farewell.

The stay in Edmonton was cut short and on the first of February I was posted to Trenton, Ontario, to take a course in administration. That again was a short stay as we were rushed through in six weeks and, lo and behold, I found myself on a train headed back to Vancouver with instructions to report to the Ford plant on Kingsway in Burnaby.

The plant had been leased to the R.C.A.F. to serve as a depot for the storage and distribution of all parts and supplies to coastal installations, being identified as No. 2 Equipment Depot. I was one of the originals of the group to serve in the unit and set up the facility. There were no barracks and everyone had to live out, renting rooms or suites in the vicinity. My case was easy as all I had to do was move in at home. It was no different from that which had prevailed when working in the Purchasing Department, regular days and hours, just having to commute a little further and wear a uniform rather than civilian clothes.

By 1943 the Ford plant was soon filled to capacity and the RCAF leased a parcel of land then known as the Kitsilano Indian Reserve, now occupied by the Planetarium, the Archives and all the land known as Vanier Park. On this they erected a group of warehouses as an enlarged facility with the site also becoming home to No. 9 Construction and Maintenance Unit operating up and down the coast of British Columbia. As this became available, the move was under way and as a result our job at the Ford plant expired with the spring of 1943. A half dozen of our staff went to the new facility and the rest of us were spread out through postings up and down the coast from Patricia Bay in the south to the Aleutians in the north.

For me the trip started by Union Steamships to Prince Rupert. We stopped at every bay and cove up the coast, with that first stage taking seven days. One night was spent at the Seal Cove Base and then I boarded an RCAF supply boat, the ex-fish packer Reel Fisher, for the trip across Hecate Strait to Alliford Bay, which was another eight hours on the high seas.

At this time in early 1943 the Japanese forces were making their intrusions into the North Pacific and made a landing on the island of Attu on 11 May. This led to immediate and urgent deployment of military forces to installations in the Aleutian chain of islands, which in part led to the start of the Northwest Staging Route, eventually to become the Alaska Highway.

At Alliford Bay the operation had some Canso aircraft searching in the Pacific for Japanese approaching the coast, particularly as a result of the submarine shelling off the coast of Vancouver Island. I was totally misplaced in Alliford Bay as they had no need for administration and was therefore placed into a crash course of aerial photography. Our equipment was primitive and it only took a matter of a few days to become considered proficient. I therefore found myself bound for Dutch Harbor. We went into the North Pacific to confront the enemy. My role was to ride the rolling and gyrating aircraft and lean into the side blister to photograph Japanese installations on Attu and thereafter on Kiska Island. This was all very well except for weather conditions that were perhaps normal but certainly deplorable as far as I was concerned. Patrols usually had a duration of anything from 8 to 14 hours and when we returned to an open and available base it was considered mission accomplished.

Despite that our operating base was at Dutch Harbor, many were the times that we had to divert landing at some alternate location. Our ventures were normal until late December of 1943 when an engine problem forced a ditching as close as we could get to a rocky outcrop of the Aleutian chain. With the aircraft maneuvered as close as possible, at the last moment we scrambled for the shore. Two of our crew were lost with six of us ending upon the rocks with a few articles of survival equipment that we salvaged from the aircraft before it disintegrated on the rocky beach.

There we were on bare rocks seeking shelter among the most inhospitable surroundings that one would want for Christmas. That was only the beginning of our ordeal. We were there for the month of January, a period of inclement weather, surviving on the salvaged emergency rations, watching a couple of our crew mentally deteriorate as the days went by. We waited and watched until a day in late January when an aircraft in relatively clear weather made a sighting and duly reported our presence. It was not more than 24 hours later a naval vessel was standing off shore to pick us up, but the weather forced him to stand a couple of miles away. There he stayed looking at us as we assembled on a prominent point looking at him. Aircraft came over and dropped us food that was most welcome, but the matter of a rescue depended on the weather and we were the victims of its vagaries.

On the 15th of February we were picked up, taken to Dutch Harbor and flown to Alliford Bay, transferred to another aircraft and flown to a hospital at Jericho Beach in Vancouver. Upon the completion of medical examinations, each of us was given a transportation warrant to the available military hospital nearest his home. With me it was simple, as I was granted 30-day leave and sent home. Others went their own way and it is unfortunate that I have never again met any of my partners on that fatal flight.

My medicals at Jericho resulted in repeated 30-day leaves on military subsistence and it was mid-May before I was declared fit for further service and posted to Northwest Air Command at Edmonton. With my command of the Russian language, I became involved in the transfer of U.S. originating military aircraft flowing from the assembly plants over the route, Canada, Alaska and Siberia, to assist the Russian forces in their conflict on the Eastern Front.

Aircraft from the various U.S. plants congregated at Great Falls in Montana and then went north through Edmonton, Grande Prairie, Fort St. John, Fort Nelson, Watson Lake, Whitehorse and on to Nome where they took off for the trans-Siberian route to the front. Being fluent in Russian, I got involved in interpreting and used to shuttle up and down the route. Russian pilots came over on a DC3 and on meeting a northbound flight would exchange aircraft, taking the Mitchell Bombers and escorting fighters on their way, while the DC3 would take the Americans back to Great Falls for the next delivery. Hundreds of aircraft were channeled through this medium and I became very familiar with not only the main airports but also all the enroute alternates, such as Smith River, Beaton River, Snag, Aishiak and Teslin.

That was the extent of my contribution to the war effort, except for one outstanding highlight when with my Russian capability I acted as an interpreter for the Russian Foreign Minister V. Molotov[1] on his transit through that same Northwest Staging Route to attend the San Francisco conference of 1945 for the drafting of the Charter of the United Nations.

During my stay in Edmonton, with that railway pass in my pocket, on every opportunity I jumped on the first available train and headed for Conoka, from there to hitch hike out to Homeglen and the farms. Those were visits long to be remembered. I felt right at home among some of my school day friends and the familiar countryside. One trip stands out in my memory when on return to Edmonton I felt ill and uncomfortable. Reporting to Medical, established a case of measles and I ended up in hospital in isolation for two weeks.

With the end of the European conflict in 1945, all efforts were now directed to the Pacific. While I volunteered, there were limited requirements and with all the returning Air Force personnel from Europe, I was now put back into administration to work on the process of their discharges. Here, release from the service naturally favored quick and efficient handling of those with overseas combat service. Being on the rear end of the stick and no European combat to my credit, being stuck in administration, my turn for release did not come until May of 1946, long after the surrender of Japan and the termination of the conflict.

---

[1] Vyacheslav Mikhailovich Molotov, March 9, 1890 – November 8, 1986. Soviet politician, diplomat, and "Old Bolshevik". A leading figure in the Soviet government from the 1920s. A protégé of Joseph Stalin. Chairman of the Council of People's Commissars (Premier) from 1930 to 1941, and as Minister of Foreign Affairs from 1939 to 1949 and from 1953 to 1956.

Top: Alec's squad, he is second from left.
Middle: B17 bomber, wrecked (not the plane Alec was assigned to).
Bottom: B17 Bomber Alec photographed on base.
Roberta Sonolet collection.

The Railroad Years

On my release in May, it was my intention to take a month or so to decide where I wanted to go and what I was going to do in the future. Much to my surprise, on the day after my release there was a phone call from Canadian Pacific Purchasing wanting to know when I was coming back to work. That settled everything and two days later I was back in the office I had left in 1941.

There was an underlying desire to follow my father in railroading and as there was no better alternative at my fingertips, I resigned myself to accepting the position of a steno-clerk with a salary of $125 per month. This was just great. With that kind of money I was a well-paid man. Since the war had ended and the tenancy provisions came to an end, we were able to get possession of our house and moved from the suite to 2906 West 5th Ave.

Now, that was a change that could be related to going from the farm to a suite. Now we were in a position of having space to spare, living room, dining room, kitchen and den, plus another three bedrooms on the second floor. We did a lot of renovations, sanding floors, painting and plumbing, upgrading to make the premises into the best that we had known since our arrival in Canada.

In 1948, for my annual vacation, I set my sights on a visit to the Montreal Purchasing headquarters to have a look at their operation and at the same time visit New York. The railway pass was a convenient fringe benefit not only providing free passage on CP Rail but also good on the American systems, such as the New York Central, Great Northern or Union Pacific that had interchange agreements with CP. New York had a special attraction since my cousin Sonja, that I had last seen on departure from Harbin, was now residing there with her husband Oscar Benz.

That was quite a visit. I stayed with them at their apartment adjacent to Greenwich Village and explored the city from one end to the other. We had night-long discussions of the events in our lives over the 23-year intervening period.

The work in purchasing became more interesting as I progressed and there was no doubt in my mind that this was where I wanted to stay. What's more, the railway was one stable factor that was there to stay and in no way a venture that could expire and leave me out on a limb looking for another vocation. In 1948 the move was on entering the era of dieselization and that was my initial introduction to the petroleum aspects. My first encounter came through the purchasing required to establish the facilities to supply the locomotive with fuel, working closely with McIntosh Supply that was the prime contractor for the installations throughout the B.C. District.

In the meantime through amalgamation of various bush operations, Canadian Pacific had become involved in air transport through a subsidiary to be known as Canadian Pacific Airlines operating out of headquarters in Edmonton in 1942. They subsequently moved to Winnipeg and in 1948 came to Vancouver.

This move brought a new phase of purchasing into the office. We were handling every requirement of all branches of CP and there were traditional guidelines to be observed. We did the purchasing from sources in our area and when suppliers happened to be in another jurisdiction such as Alberta, Manitoba or Ontario, the requisitions were forwarded to the respective Purchasing Agent for supply arrangements. Now we had a demand for provisioning that was not only from the eastern sources but also spread all over the USA.

The airline move to the coast was directed toward establishing a Canadian Pacific presence on the Pacific, as their ships lost in the war were not to return. It was now that I first became involved with the airline demands and as their requirements escalated so did the turmoil in the office. The airline required a strange range of parts and materials and as demands multiplied so did the disruption of our office routine.

On discharge from the military everyone was entitled to a rehabilitation grant based on length of service that could be claimed for various purposes. While some used it for tuition fees or trade training, others bought plots of land through what was called the Veterans Land Act. For myself I elected to use it to help with a down payment on a house. After all, I was now earning $200 per month and it was time to start looking for investments.

It was in the spring of 1949 when Capilano Properties was being developed as a new subdivision and I set my sights on a three bedroom bungalow at 3196 St. Annes Drive. This was scheduled for completion by the first of August at the grand price of $7,800. My down payment was the rehabilitation grant, with payments including principal, interest and taxes of $42 per month. On gaining possession I immediately leased the premises to a West Vancouver teacher for one year at $100 per month.

In the fall of 1949 an ex-RCAF threesome, myself, Eric Treasure and Les Taylor, in our normal visitation to the local dance halls one Saturday night ended up at the YWCA. That is one night that will not be forgotten, as there I met one Betty Marilyn Haverstock, taking her home after the dance. Her home was on 25th Ave. and Cypress St. and we used the

Marpole inter-urban line along Arbutus which at that time of night meant I had a one hour wait for the tram return to take me home. This all prompted an invitation to the house and a lengthy conversation of my New York experiences, only to be confronted by her father about the time of night. To my consternation, here I was face to face with the teacher who had so influenced my premature departure from Kitsilano HS, who was now proceeding to eject me from his house.

Just to show how persistent I could be, in work or recreation, I was entranced with that female from day one and despite the ejection called on her again. As matters developed, on Christmas of 1949 we were engaged to be married, setting a date in September 1950.

April 1950 brought sadness to the family when my sister succumbed to cancer still in the confines of the mental institution at Essondale at the age of 42. She enjoyed only the life spent in the orient, as all subsequent years after immigrating to Canada, the remaining years, were all strictly toil and strain. Her illness was a direct result of the strain in a new world and she never had an opportunity to enjoy any of the fruits of her labors.

Betty Haverstock and Alec Noble.
Roberta Sonolet collection.

Alec rides a Harley.
Roberta Sonolet collection.

My Domestic Life

We were married as planned on the 9th of September 1950 and with due consideration from my employer was elevated to a salary of $241.24 per month. The ceremony took place at Canadian Memorial Church at 15th Ave. and Burrard Street with a reception at the Hollies that were then located on the Crescent in Shaughnessy. I had arranged for a rented car for our honeymoon which was to be spent at one of her uncles' cabins on Lake Crescent in the Olympic Peninsula of Washington state.

On return to Vancouver the lease on my house on St. Annes Drive, having expired on the 31st of August, provided us with a house to move into. That was my first experience and lesson with tenants. The floors, only one year old, were a disaster. I will never know what they had moved around to make the deep scratches nor could they have worn anything but hob-nailed boots to incur the damage that was done. It took some sanding and hard work to restore the finish before they could again be considered respectable.

Of course we had little in effects and had to do with what we could afford. The war shortages of materials were still prevalent and our kitchen had to be satisfied with a two element hotplate.

My position in Purchasing through our association with McLennan, McFeely and Prior managed to get us both a Fridgidaire stove and refrigerator. In those days of consumer product shortages it was not unusual to wait for months or even a year to get a household appliance and under those circumstances we had to consider ourselves very lucky.

The first problem arose on the appliances being delivered only to find that the specifications for the house only provided for a 60 Amp service to the house. This level was not enough to meet the appliance demands. In my ignorance I had bought a pig in a poke. There was no claim on the contractor and we as a result had an electrician at our expense change the circuit capacities.

Being in a new subdivision, we had the planting of a lawn ahead of us and only sand and gravel to work with. Fortunately, with my association in the office, I had become acquainted with Alf Thistle, the operator of the CPR Gardens at 20th Ave. and Trafalgar St. In those days that was an area of relatively vacant land subject to development and the Gardens were about to leave the area for Richmond.

It must be added here that Betty had an uncle Cyril who was at the time Airport Manager at Port Hardy, and on his visits to Vancouver had the need of an automobile. He purchased a new Pontiac from Bowell-McLean on Burrard and, rather than store it in some warehouse during his absences, placed it in our garage for our use and maintenance.

With Alf Thistle having given me access to a mound of soil and on the renting of a small trailer, using the car we embarked on a hauling program to start a lawn.

We had a driveway along the side of our house to the garage in the rear and with the best of intentions embarked on a log barrier to form a curb, making space for a flower bed. For the curb, all we had to find was suitable logs and with the clearing going on for Capilano Highlands in the adjacent area, we had no problem. We would search out a suitable piece, use a rope to tie one end on the back bumper and drag it home. There were hazards involved, like the time when our prized possession let loose of the vehicle on our crossing of Queens Ave. and I had to scramble to lift the log off the street to make clearance for traffic that was coming down the street.

That was only one of the hazards of building that curb along the driveway. I next embarked on placing the logs and holding them in position by drilling each at 6-foot intervals, laying them in line and anchoring the positions with 3-foot lengths of ¾-inch pipe driven into the ground. All went well and the curb was in position except for the end piece at the street when things went wrong. Driving the last anchoring pipe, it became obstructed and in my mind assuming another rock, taking an extra heavy swing with my sledge hammer, it was very much to my surprise that the piece of pipe I was using became a conduit for a stream of water going up six feet into the air. It was my good fortune to have driven the anchoring stud right through the water supply line to the house. Thereafter it took some digging to find a shut-off and before that was done I had a flow of water the length of the block and nothing in our house. That was just another element of being a green horn home owner.

A year after we moved into the house, there was another incident worthy of mention. Our house had a rough cedar siding on the lower half and I embarked on renting spray equipment to apply a new and sparkling finish. While working on the front and getting to the end of a wall, I needed Betty to move the tank equipment trailing behind, calling for her help. Unbeknown to me, she happened to be just around the corner and on showing her face around the corner, with my coming to the end of the wall, I sprayed her face a deep forest green. There were only two eyes visible and after due cleaning, I was left to finish the job without further assistance.

That summer of 1951, on taking my vacation, we used our railway pass for a visit to the Montreal purchasing headquarters then New York to visit with my cousin Sonja.

Raisa, Tanja and Sonja were the three cousins I left behind in Harbin when we left China in 1925. She had in due course made her way to Shanghai and there married Oscar Benz, a member of the Swiss trade delegation. When World War II disrupted the normal commerce they were fortunate with their Swiss passports to flee to his homeland. After a short stay in Switzerland, they made their way to New York and became landed immigrants. At the time of our visit they were both employees of corporations in the city, with a home in Queens that we made our headquarters.

It was now an opportunity to explore again the greatest city on earth and we made the most of the opportunity. For the first time we saw television on display at RCA Centre along with all the sights that we had time for and could afford. Returning we travelled the U.S. route, New York, Chicago, Seattle and then up to Vancouver.

While I commuted to work at the station, Betty worked for R.S. Day Insurance and our combined income made us comfortable, especially since our mortgage payments were only $45 per month which included principal, interest and taxes. Betty changed jobs and went to work at the Bay Department Store for the Christmas season of 1951.

That Christmas we acquired our first dog "Raffles," an English springer spaniel, from Mr. and Mrs. Busby, an English couple who lived and bred the breed in Abbotsford. They had brought their stock with them from England and it was of prime quality attested by the ribbons and prizes they acquired at every dog show. Our acquisition of that puppy followed the tradition; we had a superior dog that warranted a propagation. Our friends Ray and Florence Brown owned an excellent mate and with their cooperation, we were to breed and raise English springers for the next 20 years. Our proliferation of the breed had to come to an end when the remaining available partners had ancestral relationships that could result with in-breeding problems. For the time being we had our original dog Raffles and a son of hers. They were the greatest pets we ever owned and lived with us for a number of years.

While we were both happy and comfortable in our house, a problem arose in July of 1952 when, along with three others from the office, we were to be loaned from the office to organize a Purchasing Department for the airline at the airport. After all, the airline and its demands were so out of the normal routine that it could no longer fit in with the railway sedate manner of business.

The mere suggestion of going out to work in a surrounding of aeroplanes after my experiences in the air force was a revolting development to say the least. After all, the railroad was fixed onto ground, it had proven a reliable transport system, my father was a railroader and, as far as I was concerned, the stability of the establishment was the place for me. To persuade management for a reconsideration was futile. They were convinced my previous experience was paramount to Canadian Pacific and the best place to exploit that was at the airport with the airline. In due course it was resolved by my acceptance of the fact that my tenure would be limited to a loan basis only and once the purchasing was all established, I would be returned to the station and the railway. All four of us were of the same understanding and, while we went to work at the airport, we remained on the railway payroll.

Top: Alec and Betty with Raffles
Bottom: Alec enjoying some time off fishing
Beverly Belanger collection

The Airline Years

Now with my assignment to the airport, the matter of commuting to Sea Island was out of the question and as a result of the requirement for transport, we borrowed $1,500 from my friend George Fazackerly and bought an Austin A-40 sedan. The car expenses were another strain on our budget and the continued operation was possible only as a result of my being made a senior clerk with a salary of $300 per month. Even with this, going to work in the mornings, with the toll on the Lions Gate Bridge, was not only costly but also lengthy. With the old Marpole Street Bridge, the antiquated Granville Street Bridge and then the Lions Gate with its toll, it was common to take two hours to get home.

Those of us from the railway office were duly joined by J.A. Mooney, transferred from Montreal where he had been on aircraft provisioning. With him and a couple of girls, we set about our task now to provide the airline without upsetting the entire traditional railway routine.

We assumed the purchasing function with the intention of hiring and training new people in the methods and procedures. With them becoming capable, we would in turn be released and return to the railway. This in due course had Sam Johnson and Archie Currie leave, however Wylie Simcox and myself remained. No sooner than we trained one person, a requirement for two more developed. We were thus to remain on that fictional loan basis paid by the railway until

1958, when all prospects of return faded and we were absorbed by the airline with transfer backdated to 1953. It might be appropriate to add here that my concept had altered and seeing major prospects there was no hesitation on my part in accepting the fate a compli.

That first winter at the airport was particularly bad for both snow and cold temperatures which made me take into consideration a move to a better proximity. It so happened that we had a New Year's invitation to a party from Alf and Gladys Thistle (the CPR garden operator) to their home at 959 Patterson Rd. in Richmond on the eve of 1952-53. While Betty and Gladys were in the living room, with Alf and I supposedly fixing drinks for them, we were having some on our own. Our conversation revealed that he had this home on property 200 feet wide and 300 feet deep, house, four-stall stable, chicken house, pig pen, another three out buildings, 14 fruit trees and a grape arbor, all this located on half of the property, using the other portion as pasture for his saddle horses.

He now informed me that as nice as it was it was too small for him and that he would like to sell, moving to larger acreage where he could go into the raising of race horses. The property description was like music to my ears and seemed a most ideal place for us, 20 minutes from downtown and 10 minutes from the airport. All of a sudden we got serious and, sitting at the kitchen table over another drink, the conversation was both short and conclusive.

"Well, Alf, if you are interested in selling this place, I just might be interested in buying."

"Yes, it's time I moved to more room. This place cost me ten and a half thousand a couple of years ago and I should get something better than that now."

"Yes, that sounds reasonable, but, since I don't have any money, I'll offer you a deal. I'll put my house in North Vancouver up for sale at a current reasonable market level and whatever I get for it, I'll pay you for this property."

"O.K., that sounds reasonable."

"The deal is made?"

"Yes."

At this stage, Gladys came in search of their refreshment that we were supposedly preparing and evidently overheard the end of our conversation. Rushing back to the living room, she advised Betty that the two drunks in the kitchen were up to no good, acting in a totally irresponsible manner. This brought them both to the scene of the negotiations and another short conversation, with Alf and I both having difficulty focusing our eyes upon these two intruders.

"Gladys, I just sold the house."

"Betty, you better go have a look around. I just bought this place."

Our wives, exited, completely bewildered and surprised by the developments and, with reservations as to the consequences, decided to leave matters alone for resolution in a later state of sobriety. There was no escape. I had become accustomed to word of mouth deals over the telephone that were not susceptible to modification or reversal. That was a tradition I followed all my life and became an element of reputation where, in telephone commitments involving million dollar deals, good or bad, you lived with the word of mouth agreement. The detail of putting factors in writing came secondary and only when time permitted for the satisfaction of the legal department.

The matter of that drunken New Year's Eve became a fact when we sold our North Vancouver house and finalized purchase of the Richmond property from Alf Thistle. The price was $11,500, a direct reflection of my selling price, and on the first of April 1953 we moved. Part of the cash payment received went to pay back the loan on our Austin A40 and what was left over went to Alf as the down payment.

This change in location was very convenient for my work and gave me the sense of being on a farm again. We immediately acquired a flock of chickens and with my hands and feet again in soil, I was in my glory with the orchard and a garden full of vegetables. That in itself meant hand labor, but our primary immediate requirement was a power mower to cut nearly half an acre of lawns. This we bought for $89 at Eaton's Department Store and, as I sit here today in 1990 writing this account of my life, that mower is still with me performing just as well today as it did when purchased. It has a Briggs and Stratton engine that has not only cut grass over the years, it has worked running a pump when our Richmond house used to flood in the heavy winter rains and in the dry summer months again drove a pump drawing ditch water to irrigate the garden.

We had plans for our extended property and felt we could get a pony. After all, we had both a stable and a pasture. The vegetable garden and flower beds were massive, to say the least, and the crops from the orchard meant we were always looking for a willing taker.

In our second year in what had been assumed as a well-established basis our dreams were shattered one day by a visitor from the Provincial Highways Department. Unbeknown to us, the decision had been made to build the Oak Street Bridge, and on showing us the proposed road drawings, it was revealed that the back portion of our property was to be expropriated for road allowances, leaving us only 130 feet of depth out of our original 300. That meant the loss of the stable, the chicken house, the pig pen and part of the orchard as well. It was a disappointment; however, the bright side must be considered since the compensation of $5,500 meant that we were only out of pocket $6,000 and still had a house on 200 feet of frontage on Patterson Rd. even though it was now to be only 120 feet deep.

During the course of all these changes in our domicile, it became a practice of spending our vacations on hunting expeditions to Alberta for all sorts of the available birds. After all, we had Raffles, the springer spaniel, a true and avowed hunter-retriever. Our partners were Gene and Jess Brown on the trips to Vulcan, Brooks and other Alberta hunting areas, which in themselves gave Betty and me a chance once more go back to Homeglen, the site of my childhood. She then, for the first time, saw for herself the fields and open spaces that were so much a part of my background.

With my sister having passed away in 1950 and my having married and gone to live away from home, these circumstances must have been difficult for my parents now in a big house all by themselves. Father had by now quit work and their only income was a small old-age pension plus whatever I had to spare that could be diverted in their direction. In July 1954 there came to their delight a young Scottish maiden, Jean Campbell, an immigrant, looking for a place to stay. Her fiancé had surveyed premises awaiting her arrival and duly deposited her with my parents, who at the time were delighted not only for the meager revenue of renting a room but having in their house a young female who was in their estimation a replacement for a daughter that was now gone. My mother doted on little Jean and she was never a tenant but just a member of the family.

Work became more and more involved and responsible as Canadian Pacific Airlines, aside from the domestic services, acquired the more advanced aircraft and began serving Tokyo, Hong Kong, the South Pacific to Australia, Mexico and South America, and extended their services to Amsterdam in 1955, Buenos Aires in 1956 and Santiago in 1957.

Mother suffered a fatal heart attack on the 22nd of June 1956, leaving Father at that time in an advanced state of senility. It is no joking matter to consider the loss of mental capability for someone in their advancing years.

It just may be an opportune time to mention the hazards that can arise and the fact that Father, knowing very well the state of his mind, used to look back upon and joke about his misadventures.

At one stage in their living at 2906 West 5th Ave. it became a routine for him to get up in the mornings and go to a store at 4th Ave. and Bayswater St. to get fresh French bread for breakfast. On this particular day Mother asked him to buy a couple of fresh tomatoes, and when he came home, there was the bread and no tomatoes. Anxious to correct the error, he immediately set forth back to the store, selecting the fruit and came back to the cashier with his selection in hand. There having been a change, the girl looked at him with surprise and asked, "How about the bread?" "Oh, I forgot," was the answer. As a result he came home with another loaf of bread along with the tomatoes.

In another incident he had to make a trip downtown for some reason and was to take a matter of a couple of hours. He left in the morning and at four in the afternoon was still not home. Getting in at nearly seven, the questions were where had he been all day. His explanations soon made it apparent that he should not be allowed to roam at will. He had made his contact in town and then gone to a corner to await the streetcar, standing there patiently for the next 4th Ave. tram. He stood there who knows how long until he became weary and, leaning on a lamp post about to go to sleep, his head drooped only to see that there were no rails on the road for the streetcar he was looking for. As it became evident in the subsequent conversation, he was looking for the streetcar on Seymour St. when he should have been one block over on Richards.

These incidents of senility were even more evident when he now tried to shave without Mother's supervision. There was one day when he was in the bathroom to wash and shave. Having duly waited for him to come forward with no result, I was confounded to see him still in the bathroom all duly washed but having trouble getting shaved. The mirror in front of him was covered with shaving cream, not one ounce on his face and there he was still trying to move the razor on a dry face.

It was obvious, without Mother there to look after requirements he could not be left on his own. After several attempts to go and live with some of his old friends, it became a necessity to take him into our house and thereby leasing the Fifth Ave. house to Jean to be not only her home but at the same time an element of assurance that we still had the inherited property.

Father, totally lost in a world without his wife, to say the least, died of a broken heart on March 31st of 1957. In body he was as strong as an ox. The years on the farm had contributed to that physical capability, but when it came to mentality, age took its toll.

At work, with the accelerated growth of the airline industry, aircraft were about to enter a medium that I could never foresee in my days in the Air Force or in the contraptions that we were then operating. Aside from domestic locations, Canadian Pacific was now serving East Asia and the South Pacific to Australia. Initially the operation was with Canadair manufactured North Star aircraft that were in effect DC4s equipped with Merlin engines. These were soon to be replaced with DC6s. On the domestic front, the DC3 was soon followed by the Convair 240.

While we railway people were supposedly there to train a suitable staff, the requirements were so far removed from previous experience even we had to learn totally new procedures. We had, at the rail station, bought only from local sources and now that could provide only the food and some of the shop requirements. The aircraft had to be supplied from the aviation industry suppliers in California, Florida, Montreal or even England.

Jean Campbell was married to Fausto Paolla in September of 1956 and with our taking father out to live with us in Richmond, they rented the house, buying it from us in 1958.

Work became more a complicated responsibly as expenditures accelerated with Canadian Pacific Air Lines, aside from the domestic services, there were more and more flights added: Peru, Buenos Aires, Portugal and Chile.

Having sworn to stay off planes with my release from the Air Force, here I was up to my ears in the aviation industry. Today looking back on the change, it must be accepted as the most beneficial happening of my life and to this day I remain most appreciative of the decisions that were made for me.

Canadian Pacific Air logo c. 1977.
Reproduced with the permission of Air Canada

Airline Fuel Purchasing Adventures

My travels on commercial aircraft started with a trip to New Orleans and while the aircraft of the time cannot be compared with those operating today, they were a far cry from the military machines. In 1958 I became responsible for fuel supplies for all stations along with several of the other purchasing details. In subsequent years, as the fuel became a major expense, it became my sole vocation to remain such until my retirement.

Some of my early fuel experiences involved the changes from gasoline engines to turbine power of the Britannia aircraft and their requirement for kerosene. The company had a far-fetched plan to operate these from the Orient through Yellowknife to Europe. The fuel had to be at Yellowknife and, with money no object, I installed tanks and an underground hydrant system, having product shipped in from Edmonton. The end result of the effort was that not one aircraft ever went near Yellowknife and two years later I sold the fuel to the native population as domestic heater fuel, abandoning the installation.

The kerosene type fuel characteristics demanded cleanliness as to particulate matter and demanded every precaution against any water presence. These factors required sophisticated filtering equipment, the perfection which took several years to develop.

My work involved the monitoring of facilities that were our suppliers and my first crisis arose when one of our aircraft had engines malfunctioning on a flight northbound out of Mexico City. Engines started to fail one after the other and the aircraft landed at Salt Lake City on an emergency basis with only one engine at full power.

The ramifications of such an incident are incalculable. The immediate investigation revealed water in the fuel tanks. The aircraft was drained and serviced, returning safely to Vancouver to be the subject of an extensive investigation.

Reg Tate, an engineer, and I were on the next flight to Mexico and on checking their facilities could not detect the source of the problem. Our next move was planned for Lima where the flight had originated to check for any possible failure at that point. Here came the point of another experience I would prefer not to have had.

Having finished our day's work in Mexico City, we elected to go to bed early to get some sleep before catching our southbound flight to Lima at 3:30 in the morning. That was all very well and good, having the best intentions for the morrow. Going to bed early in the evening was not normal and sleep would just not come. At midnight I was still tossing and turning and at about 1:00 a.m., just as the state of euphoria was setting in, an earthquake struck.

The bed started to shake, then slide from side to side. Beside me was a clothes cupboard and with each swing of the door, the automatic light flashed on and off. I lay flat on my back on the bed waiting for the ceiling to crack, in which event I was ready to go under the bed for shelter. There were noises in the hallway as people rushed out of their rooms, but I remained. In a couple of minutes all motion ceased, followed by a dead silence. Reg, having gone through the same in the next room, came in and following a short discussion, we elected to get ready and go out to the airport, as sleep was now out of the question.

We looked out the window only to see all the hotel inhabitants milling about in the park across the street, pointing and looking up at those two saps up there still on the sixth floor. It didn't take us long to get down to the lobby where we found people milling about in all states of attire being served complimentary coffee. With our bags in hand, the only comment we drew was "you're really taking this serious," to which we just nodded our heads and made a hasty exit.

In the taxi to the airport we saw some rubble and a lot of glass on the streets, with vast areas of darkness with no electricity. We found the airport closed and although our aircraft was there, our departure was delayed an hour while the runways were inspected. We finally departed and were on our way to Lima.

At home Betty heard news reports about the earthquake in Mexico and in an effort to verify my welfare started a series of telephone calls, only to be advised, "Don't worry about him. He's in Lima."

Our search in Lima was fruitless and two days later we were back in Mexico City. We persisted with our suspicions and despite the wrath of airport authorities and Aero Servicios, the fuel handlers, three days later we found a discrepancy between the engineering drawings and the actual installation. A water draw-off valve had not been installed where required, allowing water to flow with the fuel, further complicated by the fact that their water detection system was deficient.

A report of our findings was duly filed with the Minister of Civil Aviation which resulted in major changes at Mexico

City. The incident proved the necessity for a more vigilant monitoring of procedures that were subsequently introduced at other locations.

With some of the disasters that befall an airline operation, it sometimes makes one wonder how they survive. Buying an aircraft is unlike anything else. With a car it's a simple matter. The vehicle is there to see, the price can be negotiated and you drive away with your purchase. With a sophisticated aircraft, the manufacturer firstly promotes an engineering concept of performance. Should this meet the proposed customer's demand, a sale contract can be completed. However, since different operators have different ideas as to the planned operations they have in mind, their demands vary. Boeing, Douglas, Lockheed or any other manufacturer leaves open the option as to the engines to be installed as just one of the many such items. It now becomes the buyer's responsibility to purchase and deliver the engines to be installed. After all, if they already have established shops and a spare parts inventory for a particular type, a bastard with its particular demands would be most undesirable. The same now comes into play when it comes down to all the electronics. Having Bendix, why introduce Sperry or another make? This carries on through the seats, the upholstery, the galley equipment, right down to the paints and decals to be applied.

Once the sale purchase agreement has been signed, the aircraft manufacturer provides a list of the optional items to be supplied for his installation, along with the dates on which they are to be delivered to his plant. The conditions can create havoc for purchasing, as any failure in the schedule means the aircraft is shunted off the assembly line and will have to wait for an opening to get back in.

In 1962 when Canadian Pacific agreed to purchase DC8 aircraft from the Douglas Corp. of Long Beach, it was elected that we would use Rolls Royce engines. Douglas built the aircraft and we were left with them standing on a Douglas tarmac as Rolls failed to meet the delivery schedule. We had people out to beg, borrow or steal any spare engines that could be found at other Rolls operators and when successful chartered aircraft to fly them to Long Beach. It was, of course, all resolved and the delayed aircraft arrived, but it was the last time that Rolls Royce was to be considered.

With my employment in the airline, our vacations took a new concept and instead of Alberta, we took off for the international field. Our first was spent in Mexico City and the Hacienda Vista Hermosa in the Cuernavaca Valley, the one-time country retreat of the Emperor Maximillian. In 1963 we spent a vacation in Japan and subsequently made trips to Europe.

A Noble
Director Fuel Purchasing

CPAir
One Grant McConachie Way
Vancouver International Airport
British Columbia, Canada V7B 1V1
Tel (604) 270-5245 Res (604) 263-7958
Telex 043-55587 SITA YVRPPCP

Vancouver Airport Fuel Facilities Corporation

One Grant McConachie Way
Vancouver International Airport
British Columbia V7B 1V1
Tel: (604)263-7958

A. Noble
President

Alec's business cards

Alec at work.
Beverly Belanger collection

A Visit to Moscow

The highlight of travels came in 1962 when on September 13th I left bound for Moscow with the arrangement that Betty would meet me in London on the 22nd. That developed into a once in a lifetime experience.

On my departure I had my passport and visa, prepaid hotel, prepaid car and chauffeur for three hours each day and three meal tickets for each day of my proposed stay. Formalities on my arrival by KLM from Amsterdam were minimal except for the money in my possession, Canadian, U.S., Dutch and English. This all had to be counted and listed in detail on a special exchange form that was to be presented when Rubles were purchased, each transaction was to be recorded and any money in my possession at departure would have to be balanced therewith.

My cousin Raisa met me at the airport, our meeting being the first since I left Harbin in 1925. The assigned chauffeur was there for me at the front door and we duly proceeded to the Ukraina Hotel, my residence for the stay. This initial entry into the hotel relieved me of my passport for unknown reasons with the remark that it could be reclaimed the next day. The room was of an acceptable standard on first appearances and it was to my chagrin to later learn that the bed either had bed bugs or fleas, which feasted on me every night that I was there.

Without delay we made our way to her apartment where she resided with her daughter Irena, a son-in-law and a grandchild in three rooms and a bathroom. It was now learned that my aunt Zina, my mother's sister, had passed away and the first two days were practically all devoted to catching up on our divergent events of the 37 years of our separation.

While an accounting for me was relatively simple, theirs, on the other hand, having remained in China was a different story. My aunt's husband, Mr. Sergunin, had passed away shortly after our departure and with progressive Chinese assumption of the railway, there was little for any of the Russian population to do. My cousin Raisa married a Dr. Yasinsky and with him being independent of the railway, they lived quite well. They had one daughter, Irena, and remained in Harbin until after World War II and the passing of the doctor. Sisters Sonja and Tanya went to live in Shanghai in the 30s to eventually suffer the Japanese occupation and the effects of the war. Tanya married a Russian engineer, raising two sons, Georgie and Vladimir, while Sonja, as mentioned earlier, married Oscar Benz, a member of the Swiss trade delegation.

In 1948 the Communist regime made it most uncomfortable for any foreigner in the country and all had to seek refuge and life elsewhere. Sonja and Oscar had it easy. With his Swiss citizenship, at the first opportunity they departed for Switzerland. From there he was appointed to the trade delegation in New York and that is where Betty and I had visited them, as I did on many following visits to New York during the course of my business travels. It was also through them that the Moscow contacts were established resulting in my deciding to make the Moscow visit.

The remainder of the family, Raisa, her mother Zina, daughter and son-in-law, Tanya and her family applied for acceptance as immigrants to Australia, Canada and the U.S.A., only to be declined. As the only alternative being of Russian origin, they obtained visas for Russia (USSR), being their only escape from Chinese persecution. They spoke of many hardships in their journey and finally made their new homes with Raisa and family in Moscow, while Tanya settled in Tula, a city some 175 km to the south.

My visit was an experience to remember. We wined and dined every night and, with my car and driver, we went sightseeing every day at their direction and knowledge of the points of interest. This all led to some incidents that one could only experience in Moscow.

One evening, having played cards until 2:30 in the morning, they came with me onto the street to find a taxi to take me back to the hotel. As we stood on the curb, the first car stopped and beckoned me in, only to have the relations immediately step in saying, “Don’t take that car, he is just an entrepreneur having a car in effect scalping in off hours, driving to gain revenue, is not licensed, does not have a meter and is liable to be asking for exorbitant charges.” We therefore waited for a legal taxi.

The next experience to demonstrate the difference between socialism and private enterprise arose one evening when we were busy with another card game. There came a knock on the apartment door. Raisa answered then came back motioning for her son-in-law to go to the kitchen. We sat and waited to continue the game, me with ears egging to understand the faint conversation that could be heard. Was it the KGB or the local police there to inquire about entertaining a foreign visitor and were they or I going to be in trouble?

The interruption only lasted 15 or 20 minutes and he came back to the table to casually resume the game. I was bewildered and obviously seeing the look on my face he came forth with a clarifying statement.

"That was the tailor from the shop where I bought a suit last week. He came over to take a note of the adjustments to be made so that he can do the work at home. I will pay him rather than have it done in the shop where the money would go to the state and he would get only his normal salary." It was just another display of private enterprise.

Our conversation one evening disclosed that they were very familiar with my godmother who had been one of those to remain in Harbin on our departure from China. She had stayed there through the war years, immigrating back to Russia at the same time as they did, settling in Sverdlovsk, some 15-16,000 km to the east of Moscow. They had a number where she could be reached and without deliberation it was decided to phone her.

That decision was another experience when compared with the quick and simple convenience of long distance calling at home. Here we had to go to the local telephone exchange to place an order at a wicket where the particulars of my requirement were duly recorded and the question was asked, "When do you want this completed and for how long?" To me it was a somewhat bewildering question and on requesting "now," I was informed that was impossible. The attendant handed me a bill for the proposed call to be paid to a cashier and on returning with a receipt for 15 minutes, we negotiated for the event to take place at 8 a.m. the next day. The exercise took 45 minutes and they finally agreed to make the connection to my hotel room rather than having to come back to the telephone exchange at the appointed connection time.

True to their promise, the phone rang in my room on time and there was my godmother on the other end. I will leave out the details of our conversation except for one factor in that she decided before our conversation was over to see me despite my scheduled departure at 3 p.m. the next day. I attempted to discourage her but to no avail and she arrived in Moscow before the day was over. Now an elderly lady of nearly 80, she was spry and healthy, which made our meeting, though short, one of the most pleasant that one could expect.

During my roaming through the stores of the city, I was fascinated with not only their procedures of retailing but also the fact that separate establishments handled meat, dairy products, vegetables, bakery products or other items. In them all payment was required first and with a receipt in hand, one could now go to a counter and pick up what had been paid for.

Food in restaurants was fair to good but the service left a lot to be desired, even the hotel, although of the first class category could, by western standards, only be considered mediocre.

On one occasion sitting in the dining room, a party at another table raised the complaint of a scrap of food on a chair. The waitress did not come to their request for cleaning but merely threw them a cloth with the remark, “If you don’t like it, wipe it up.”

Being accepted as one of the family, my relatives spoke with me in the most informal terms. They condemned many of the policies and methods being adopted by the regime. While acknowledging that conditions had improved with the Krushev regime, they did not hesitate to make known that further changes were the objective of the population.

One element that they were very liberal in talking about was the inefficiency of industry and its failure to meet domestic demands for living comforts. They were liberal in their complaints about the expenditures on military objectives and at the same time condemned the socialist system that so lacked personal initiative. There was one instance where we went to a hotel for dinner only to see three attendants at the coat and hat check counter when by our stands one would have been under employed. When asking why the surplus of manpower was in effect entertained, the simple answer was that rather than having the aged sit at home and be welfare recipients, it was sociologically better to give the individuals a sense of serving and the personal satisfaction of performing a service for the state.

In my conversations with the people who were above the unskilled labor class, those who had degrees and specialized education status, advanced opinions that the socialist structure left much to be desired.

In 1962 during my visit there were frequent complaints about the spending on military technology, the lack of concern for the populace and particularly the lack of domestic comforts. Now in 1990 as I write my memoirs with the introduction of Glasnost, the failures of the domestic industry are becoming self-evident.

Failure of the system became obvious to me when we talked about proficiency. It was frankly admitted that an employee assigned to a manufacturing plant was placed into the job at the direction of the state. There were no avenues of getting rid of an incompetent other than the prescribing of a promotion. There were, as related to me, many cases of total incompetency and to get rid of such an individual meant documenting his/her superior abilities qualifying them for a promotion. There was no way of firing and sending one onto the street to fend for themselves.

My conversationalists were very frank to admit that those

very incompetents were in due course to flow through various enterprises with the same results. Being incompetents, each of the assigned employers followed by making recommendations as an avenue of disposal. In due course what happened was that the incompetents that had been disposed of a couple of years earlier now came back to the original place of employment in a management category. There and then the ability of industry was subject to the total inadequacy of the directing management, the incompetent.

It was very apparent to me that for previous serfs and laborers, conditions had improved. They were either being paid a meager existence salary or being placed into positions such as the coat and hat checkers at the hotels. These people having not had much in their past were easy to satisfy.

The form I had received on listing my available currency on arrival had on the reverse in bold print "It is prohibited to remove from the Soviet Union, Antiques, Items of Art, Precious Gems or Minerals, Currency and Stamps." With Betty collecting stamps, I had my eyes open for any available bargains. The assortments were there before my eyes and only the thoughts of the entry form were in the back of my mind.

On speculation I bought a few packages on the assumption that if they were taken away from me at the airport, the expense would just have to be a write-off. Another item of concern arose when my relatives insisted on my taking some U.S. currency from them to offset the cost of items they wanted me to purchase and send them as Christmas presents from Canada. Here I was now about to leave the country not only carrying prohibited stamps but also with more money that I had on my arrival.

There was only one thing to do at the airport when I was required to sign the exchange forms as to its accuracy, plead ignorance to what was all in Russian and decline to sign on the pretext that I was not aware of what I was signing. This upset the attendant and on threats of being declined exit, I signed under protest, expecting full well that they would now proceed to inspect my possessions, leading to a subsequent jailing. Much to my surprise once the forms were signed, he placed them into a box on the desk and with a broad smile motioned me to the exit gate.

That brought my Moscow visit to an end. I left on KLM to Amsterdam, changing to a flight for London and joined Betty at the Park Lane Hotel at midnight. We in due course made our way to Paris and Antwerp and Amsterdam before finding our way home again.

Alec visiting his cousins in Moscow.
Roberta Sonolet collection.

Starting a Family

The year 1963 was to change our lives forever by Beverly, born on 8 June, placed with us on 11 December and being formally adopted on 15 March 1964. We were delighted with her, however, our lack of baby care experience on the first day with us necessitated a call for help and Norma Carswell came over that evening. With the benefit of her advice, we were soon adjusted to all the new demands.

While we appreciated her presence, the affection the dog displayed was the most surprising. Our springer spaniel Butch, already an adult, would sit by her crib or carriage, guard and watch her as though she were his property. We never had to be concerned as to his whereabouts; wherever the baby was, he was there too.

Work at the office had no respect for the domestic demands. My travels became more frequent and far flung. While Moscow had been quite an education, the experiences in Ecuador were something else. I had seen the slums and poverty of Mexico and Peru but the sights in both Guayaquil and Quito were the most depressing. People worked banana plantations for a handout of food, slept on the sidewalks with rats in their midst, school and medical services were only for the wealthy. In the dry season the presence of insects was bearable, however, when the rain came, everything seemed to hatch and take flight at once. Lamp standards at night attracted a meter diameter ball of these around the light, making it barely visible. My first-class hotel had metal furnishings in the room and no rugs anywhere, as wood or fabric was susceptible to infestation and destruction.

Fuel purchasing assumed a new concept in the decade with the airlines taking over airport storage and dispensing facilities from the oil companies. Through interline agreements, this brought me into the consortium type of operations and as they proliferated so did the frequency of travel. The medium required my participation in the financing, contracting and construction as well as the operations at many of the airports that CP Air was serving at the time. Progressively my involvement in day to day purchasing of the various requirements was diminishing, however, some incidents are worthy of mention.

Like the experience with Rolls Royce, we were faced with a similar failure on the part of British industry in 1966 involving the Spode china for aircraft on-board services. It's not a simple matter of having a set to serve some 200 meals on a flight, but every item must be provided by the thousands to have sets at every station that the aircraft might visit. We were taking delivery of a fleet of DC8-63s and as a result of the Spode failure to deliver we had not so much as a cup and saucer to serve the passengers.

In a panic I left for the Noritake china plant in Nagoya, Japan, to arrange the manufacture of plates, bowls, cups, saucers and everything else to our specific design, ten thousand pieces of each item. We agreed on a delivery schedule and, true to their tradition, the Japanese performed with punctuality. Needless to say, we never again ordered a single piece of china from England.

Fortunately, the stressful instances were often offset by what could be termed as hilarious requests, like a requisition for one pair of rubber boots, both left feet, or the request for one long-boiled egg maker. On first response one would be inclined to go to the nearest poultry supply house, buy a fowl, boil it overnight for delivery the next day. Such was not the case and this long-boiled egg maker had to be brought in on a special order from a manufacturer in England. It turned out to be a stainless steel tube-like appliance into which egg whites were deposited for boiling to produce a 5-cm diameter, 35-cm long rod of cooked egg white. This would then be sliced up and cut into little stars or half-moons to be used as decoration on salads or hors d'oeuvres.

Another instance to break the monotony was a case of some 50 Chinese seamen who went on strike in the harbor. The shipping company was sending them all back to Hong Kong and brought them out to board an aircraft for the flight. At the last minute they all refused to go unless they were provided Chinese meals. Panic is the only way to describe such a situation. The kitchen came up with dishes, a truck and with me directing, we took off for Chinatown and a restaurant to get the genuine articles. Luck was with us. We got the meals and the flight departed with only a two-hour delay.

With my frequent absences, we soon realized that a half acre of lawns, the flower beds and vegetable garden were just too much to manage. In1965 we decided that our 200 feet of frontage on Patterson Road could be sub-divided and a duplex built for revenue purposes. Approvals and a mortgage were gained in short order and our project was completed in August with us moving into one half. Payments were no problem with revenues from the other half and from the old house.

While we certainly enjoyed the foreign vacations, we did not abandon our appreciation of the domestic country scene. Having acquired a Ford pick-up, we experimented with one trip to the Peach River Dam sight with a rented camper unit.

On the next opportunity we rented a trailer that we took down to Yellowstone, becoming convinced that trailering was by far superior to campers. The rental unit was typical, having only bare necessities which convinced us to seek and purchase our own unit with not only the cooking and sleeping accommodations but also heating, refrigeration and toilet. The first purchase was a 16-foot Kenskill, to be followed in due course by an 18-foot and finally a 22-foot deluxe Travelaire.

Fortune smiled on us again in 1966 when we were introduced to Roberta, born 1 February, placed with us 9 May and adopted on the 23rd of December.

With the two girls, our normal vacation routine meant taking the trailer to a park at Parksville on Vancouver Island, parking it there for the summer. Mother and the children settled in for at least a couple of months, with me joining them for weekends and my normal vacation time. It was all a very convenient arrangement and afforded me the opportunity to get in a fair share of time on the water fishing. In those days there were no licenses required for salt water nor were there any limitations on the numbers caught. It became a routine to deposit a box of fish periodically with a custom packing house in Nanaimo to have half smoked and canned, the balance just canned. For some years we therefore always had our own hoard at minimal expense.

As the children grew without interfering with the summer routine we managed to take them to Switzerland to visit Sonja in Zurich, then Disneyland and Hawaii. With all the benefits and free air transportation, the reservations held on transfer from the railway soon faded into oblivion.

In 1968 the old house was in need of some extensive repair and rather than spend the money, it was put up for sale. Having bought the original property for $11,500, sold a portion to the Province for their road for $5,500, we were still able to get $13,500 for the house and the sub-divided lot it sat on, retaining the other lot and duplex.

With the money we paid off Alf Thistle and with some savings immediately bought the house at 3073 West 35th Ave. for $25,000. I leased it out for a year and in August of 1969, with Beverly ready to start school, we moved in.

Beverly, Alec, Betty and Roberta with their beloved Springer Spaniels. Beverly Belanger collection.

Alec Noble

Traveling the World

In all my years with the airline, I can recall only four instances of bad accidents and loss of life, one being particularly distasteful to me. A demented individual managed to explode a bomb in the rear washroom of a DC6 over Williams Lake, blowing the tail off the craft. Responsibility fell upon my shoulders to arrange all the handling of the deceased with undertakers and then their dispatch to their home towns.

The operation of an airline has its hazards, fortunately many are mere stumbles and fumbles that can make one wonder just what can go wrong next. We had one instance of filling a flight with passengers, the cabin attendants had everyone seated and strapped in, the doors were closed and when they went to push the aircraft away from the terminal gate found no crew in the cockpit.

Comedy can be the name for events that can lead others to tears. An Oriental lady of advanced years with no English capability was being sent by her Toronto family on one final visit to Hong Kong. Needing assistance to get around at Vancouver she was seated into a departure area to await the Hong Kong connection two hours away. Some passenger agent noticed her and tried to communicate to no avail. He was unaware of intentions but having mentioned Toronto found this to be understood. The lady smiled and with that response was immediately bundled up and deposited on board a direct flight back to her point of origin.

The provision of meals often results in chaos in the kitchen. All prepared food goes into the special containers to fit the aircraft galley and vehicles are constantly on the move either bringing in the used and dirty equipment from arrivals as others are taking out the fresh recharges for the scheduled departures. We had one aircraft that went to Pr. Rupert and back in the morning with breakfast served. It was turned around and went right out on its second trip to Rupert, this time with a lunch on board. Much to the chagrin of staff and passengers, they found that the drivers had made a mistake with trucks and instead of lunch there was only the used and dirty breakfast dishes back on board.

Lost baggage or cargo, the subject of many jokes, can also present some frequent embarrassing situations.

There was a day when a shipping company had one of their vessels stranded in Italy with a part failure originally manufactured and supplied by a Montreal firm. We were asked to carry this on the next available flight as a priority item that must go even if a paying passenger has to be removed. On that basis they paid a double freight charge. On attempting to load the 200 kg piece, it was found that the protective crating prevented it from going through the cargo door. Without hesitating they took the protection all off, loaded the piece and then went in and put the crate together to prevent any damage from the hold-down strapping. At Rome where the plane has a two-hour turnaround, they wrestled with the shipment and, as passengers were boarding for the return flight, rather than delay a departure, closed the doors and sent it off. At Montreal the cargo crew, on opening the doors, was startled to see their masterpiece again. They now had to get it off, wait till the next day for another flight, go through the loading again and, after some communicating with Rome to clarify procedures, had it on its way again. In this case fortunately the part was not lost but it did, with its priority rating, cross the ocean three times and only took four days to get there.

In 1970 fuel consumption was increasing at an unheard of pace and at the same time so were fuel taxes. The International Air Transport Association (IATA) headquartered in Geneva had within it a branch identified as the Fuel Trade Group composed of the fuel managers from the member airlines. I was appointed as the CP representative to this group where the opportunity presented itself to meet all my counterparts and be party to the discussions of our mutual problems. This now required at least three trips a year to Geneva to attend the called meetings.

The Air Transport Association in Washington, D.C., had a similar fuel managers' group concerned only with matters confined to the U.S.A. In 1971, I was appointed as the CP representative, which now required the attendance of periodical Washington gatherings.

That was not to be the end, as in 1972, I was again the subject of an appointment as representative on the Air Transportation Association of Canada located in Ottawa. More meetings and more travel.

Alec at work.
Beverly Belanger collection.

The Fuel Crisis

The era ushered in by the 70s was to become the most trying of my times in fuel purchasing. I was now detached in total from other purchasing activities, being involved in consortium operations at numerous airports and at the same time responsible for the total fuel account for the operations. I had to present to management a budget for operating costs and was expected to forecast what changes might be expected that could reflect on profits.

It was a time ripe for total confusion. Firstly, the Arab states, rather than dealing on their own, in an unprecedented move formed the Organization of Oil Exporting Countries (O.P.E.C.). The crude producers now unified were a force to be reckoned with and did not hesitate to make their demands known. Their initial move was to demand a greater royalty on the crude being removed from their entities. Any failure in reaching a satisfactory resolution brought in some instances the next step in enforcing nationalization with minimal compensation.

Now the petroleum companies and the consuming nations were no longer dealing with individual states but with a consortium that had a common goal to maximize their revenue. The producers were well aware of the profits of the seven sisters (Exxon, Chevron, Texaco, Gulf, Mobil, Shell and B.P.). All gained at their expense and the low royalty revenues. Initial demands for increased royalties started the first stages of price escalation, as these escalated so did the confrontations. When some of these negotiations collapsed, they brought in the nationalization factor.

Transport, refining and marketing were under control of the seven sisters. When negotiations came to a standstill with the failure of OPEC to attain their demands, an embargo was enforced to prevent crude shipments to the U.S.A. This came at a time when the petroleum industry had all available storage filled to capacity. They in effect had so much crude on their hands that tankers were on the high seas acting as storage waiting for a port where they could unload. At the same time during the embargo there were cases of many ships leaving Arabian ports for the non-embargoed ports but were in fact traded from one corporation to another while at sea only to become a cargo for the embargoed ports. This not only transferred cargoes but in fact even involved the ownership of the vessels. A ship could leave with a crude cargo ex Kuwait, in mid-Atlantic its colors would change from green and yellow to blue and red, the name could change from Yellow Star to Blue Horizon port of registry from Monrovia to Liberia. Anyone trying to track these manipulations didn't have a hope and the result was that crude from the Arab states was coming into the U.S.A. despite the embargo.

While the supply of crude was flowing into the U.S.A. the seven sisters were making the most of the situation. With their lobbying capabilities, they super-imposed their influence on the authorities and, so to speak, encouraged the formation of what was to become known as the Dept. of Energy (D.O.E.).

With the Dept. of Energy under the guidance of the Petroleum Industry, they reacted to the detriment of all consumers in a program of allocations in an effort to conserve on consumption. They made some feeble efforts in reducing speed and prescribed limits on industrial consumption in general. Their first effort required industrial consumptions to 70 percent of what had been purchased and consumed the previous year. This included airlines and their demand for jet fuel.

The chaos that resulted is one that should serve as an education for the politicians in years to come and also demonstrate the fact that interference by those elected to office requires a lot more than just a superficial analysis or the capitulation to a strong lobby.

Once the petroleum industry got the administration on their side they went about setting their own rules. Firstly, customers placed on the 70 percent restriction had to average it out over 12 months to be taken as equal monthly quantities. Any allocated volume not taken in a given month was lost and could not be carried forward. This was just another oil industry pressure tactic and any product left on their hands could then be placed on the market to those without an allocation at double the normal retail price. The marketers used every angle they could imagine, all for the sole purpose of raising prices to the levels they wanted to preserve profitability regardless of the crude escalation.

Once the 70 percent factor came into play there was total chaos as a result of the progression of events. Some consumers, and I speak here only of the airlines, had changed contracted supply sources because of competitive price bidding. Now they found themselves with a contract with their chosen supplier and an allocation from the supply source of the previous year that was no longer competitive in the pricing range. That type of situation was only a fraction of all the obstacles that arose through government administration and interference. There were new carriers that did not exist in the previous year, there were new stations introduced by existing scheduled carriers that were not served the previous years or, to top it all off, some suppliers had ceased to exist and one could end up with a 70 percent allocation that amounted to zero.

The chaos introduced by the interference of elected officials was not one that had any precedent. Any requirement for a change or modification with due respect for demands required a meeting with the Dept. of Energy. I was there on repeated visits because of our particular demands.

Los Angeles was no problem because what shortages were apparent could be filled by freighting fuel on board the aircraft from Vancouver. San Francisco was another matter since we had changed from flying DC8 aircraft to 737s. The 70 percent allocation was more than we could use. On the other hand, Air Canada was in dire straits and could only get a fraction of their requirement. CP had a Vancouver-Honolulu service that was also in a predicament, while serving Honolulu three times a week in the summer, the frequency changed to 11 flights per week in the winter.

The petroleum industry setting of equal monthly uplifts introduced restrictions that were a plague on the airline efforts to maintain their services.

I had a monthly scale of consumption prescribed to me by the suppliers and at the same time could see the fact that the regulations were a total failure on the part of the administration to understand the total ramifications of their activities.

Now let me tell you how we, the consumers [the airlines], reacted. Firstly, I made a deal with Air Canada giving them access to the fuel we were not about to consume at San Francisco. Secondly and a part of the above, I agreed to accept from Air Canada the allocation they held as a result of some charter operations they had operated in the previous year to Honolulu. So now we traded for our mutual benefit, but that was not the end of the story. It was only one stage in the fuel shortages and restrictions on consumption.

Now to maintain operations and looking to the future, I elected to make a deal with Singapore Airlines. They were one of the new carriers on the Pacific that had no allocation but were in the process of purchasing a cargo of jet fuel in Kuwait that would not be available in Honolulu until late in the year. I went to Singapore and made a deal whereby I would, in the name of Canadian Pacific, purchase allocations made on our behalf and not having a direct requirement would have it delivered into aircraft of Singapore Airlines, in effect using their aircraft as storage for allocations that we were not able to consume in the monthly level imposed by the producers.

Now I was purchasing fuel in San Francisco, giving it to Air Canada. They in turn were purchasing their allocation in Honolulu, having it delivered to CP aircraft and I was in turn purchasing my Honolulu allocation having it delivered into Singapore aircraft. The end result to all intents and purposes being that the fuel available to us in the slack summer season would now be available in our peak consumption winter months at which time Singapore would have their tanker cargo in place and would repay me the gallons supplied them from our summer month surplus.

The accounting for all this mish-mash was more than anyone could ask for. I had two clerks as my staff who were expected to manage all these deals made by me on my travels, and I was only in the office some seven days out of a month to make sure all was in order.

In this particular period I was either in meetings in Geneva, Washington or Ottawa on a regular basis. To this point I have spoken of the problems with the Dept. of Energy in

Washington and some of the contortions that were required of a consumer to make their operations successful.

All of that on the part of U.S. authorities was related directly to the panic type of reactions as a result of the escalating prices, the embargo and the petroleum industry lobby promoting the spectre of shortages.

There, in fact, were no shortages. Every available storage facility was filled to capacity either with crude or refined products. Tankers were sitting on the high seas with their cargo and no place to off load.

One of my most exasperating experiences involved CP Air operation of some ski charters from Toronto to a resort in Idaho. The aircraft required fuel for their return and the only dealer on the airport, a Texaco agent, was prevented from making a supply available on direct orders from headquarters in New York. Having no shortage of fuel in Canada, my readily available solution was to send a truck with 8,000 gallons down there, offering the agent a premium rate of five cents per gallon to store our product and dispense it to aircraft as required. The response was immediate: "Don't send anything down here. Our tanks are all full." This was just another example of the tactics of the petroleum industry to promote the shortages concept in their effort to gain the higher pricing levels they were seeking. Our problem was finally resolved through a friend at Great Falls, Montana.

While it can be said that government reactions for the protection of industry and the welfare of the population can be justified, there comes a time when a panic response with a strong lobby promotion must be condemned. The U.S. Dept. of Energy in typical American style overreacted.

Some of the meetings I attended in Washington dealt with the possibility of replacing the embargoed crude through the gasification of coal, the refining of a petroleum product from the shales of Wyoming or the possible use of liquid hydrogen. While they were alternatives, all were prohibitively expensive unless crude reached the 50 or 60 dollar range per barrel. Since there were no assurances of such, few were willing to gamble the investments required and in due course as crude prices modified these speculative adventurous considerations fell by the wayside.

Let us not say that the Americans were the only ones to fall in the face of the petroleum industry lobby, for in Canada our National Energy Board also fell under the spell. Firstly, they came up with an atrocious energy policy when we were not subject to any embargo and had the resources to meet all domestic demand. They jumped into the fray with pricing controls on crude which resulted in suppressed pricing of the refined products and at the same time, at tax payers expense, set out to compensate oil exploration companies with a major portion of their expenses.

The first and obvious result of our suppressed jet fuel pricing opened the door to opportunism. Flights out of Los Angeles going the Polar route to Europe stopped in Winnipeg to load cheap Canadian jet fuel. So did everyone who had to transit Canadian air space. Flights from the eastern seaboard called in Montreal or Gander. Flights from Europe to Asia that normally operated through Anchorage now made a convenient detour through Edmonton, Calgary or Vancouver to pick up their fuel for the Pacific flight.

Now the suppressed fuel price was playing right into the hands of foreign carriers whether they operated in Canada or not. This all sparked another reaction that was lacking in both thought and consequences. The National Energy Board came up with the idea that Canada with its controls should not be a haven for the profit conscious foreign operators. Some bright spark on the Board came up with the idea that we in Canada should have a J.A.R.P. (just and reasonable price). Now if you should look back on the problems introduced by the interference of the Dept. of Energy in the USA they could be placed into a minor role compared to the Canadian reaction.

Firstly, at the direction of the National Energy Board the oil companies were now required to charge consuming airlines a set price per gallon regardless of their crude costs or the level of the retail market. This factor was meant to apply to any flight operated on an international basis or to any foreign carrier that came into a Canadian airport to purchase fuel. The airlines under the auspices of the Air Transport Association challenged the impositions which lead to many meeting confrontations that contained verbal confrontation that would not be appropriate for mention herein.

To put matters into a short format, let it be known that the NEB efforts were challenged by not only the domestic operators but by the foreign ones as well and in due course NEB efforts to superimpose their will on the market place came to naught. CP Air and Air Canada paid nothing into that pool and all the monies collected from the foreign carriers were in due course refunded.

This all was not the end of the NEB consideration of future consumption. As a direct reflection of US concerns, they embarked on the designing of a program of fuel allocation if such were to become a necessity. Here and now I found myself a member of the Supplies Allocation Board.

We had our meetings in Ottawa and designed a program of who would get what, where restrictions would apply and what ration cards were to be designed for the various categories that we prescribed.

This was a time when I was having my meetings with the Dept. of Energy in Washington, the Air Transport

Association of America in Washington, the International Transport Association in Geneva, the airline consortiums building fuel facilities in San Francisco, the new international terminal in Los Angeles, all aside from the fact that I was a party to the facilities in progress in Honolulu, Mirabel, Toronto, Calgary or Dorval.

CP Air Boeing 737-200 on final approach at Whitehorse, Yukon, Canada.
Photo by Terry A. Danks 1971 - Wikimedia Commons

Working 24 Hours Days

It might be said that I was at this stage a workaholic because my days, all 24 hours, were devoted to making the airline operation a success.

In the final analysis, let me say that the final years of employment were the most satisfying of my whole life in that I attained a status of reliability to the corporation and must accept that I was rewarded to the maximum that the corporation could extend. The fact that I had not so much as graduated from grade 10 played no role in my assessments, it was only performance. The final year of employment , 1982, my budget was 273 million dollars and, from the president down, no one ever questioned just where or how I managed the allocation. It was not unusual to pick up a phone, call a contact and by word of mouth buy a one million dollars' worth of fuel. My reputation was known and a word of acceptance was worth its weight in gold. One million dollars was just a routine transaction.

Because of the necessity of meeting at various times to compare notes and mutual problems, it was not unusual to make a phone call to Ken Brooks at Qantas in Sydney, Australia, and arrange to meet with him on a given date in Geneva for dinner. At the same time, it was also not unusual to have enroute meetings with P. Biemont of KLM in Amsterdam or F. Pedron of Air France in Paris.

No one will ever know how I scrambled to make connections

from one flight to another to meet the scheduled and arranged meetings. There were some failures and as one example, I can quote the experiences of a scheduled meeting in Geneva for Monday morning.

I left home on Saturday afternoon on a direct flight to Amsterdam, due there on Sunday to make a connection for Geneva. Unfortunately for me, Amsterdam was covered by fog and we landed in Prestwick to await a clearing. We finally got out in the afternoon and by the time we got into Amsterdam, with the day's delayed flights, there were no seats available to get on my way. I stayed overnight and on Monday found that the fog was now over Amsterdam and had also spread south so that Geneva was also closed. I had no hope of getting to Geneva for a meeting that was already in session. The end result was that I flew from Vancouver to Prestwick, to Amsterdam, back to Toronto and then to Vancouver, spending three days in the air and ending up at home in Vancouver on Monday evening, never having made it to the Geneva meeting.

In the course of my travels, this was not the only experience with travel problems. I was on one trip through South America when CP was about to introduce the Brittania aircraft and a turbine fuel requirement. To ensure fuel availability I was out on a survey and in due course visited Lima, Pisco, Antofogasto, Valpraiso, Santiago, Mendoz, Cordoba, Buenos Aires, Mar del Plata and Montevideo to set up all the fuel arrangements. Coming home I got up as far as Lima and found no seats available to go further as a result of a World Trade Fair that was at the time being held in Mexico City.

In the end result I went on Braniff from Lima to Miami, Northwest Airlines from Miami to Chicago and then United from Chicago to Seattle. Now my leaving Chicago got me into Seattle just a matter of one hour after the last flight left for Vancouver. Not being all that ready to spend another night in a hotel, from Chicago I phoned home for Betty to drive down to Seatac airport to pick me up and before the day was over, I was home in Vancouver having slept in the back of the station wagon all the way home from Seattle.

The final years with the airline were a panic from one day to another. If it was not for the Arab states and their demands, it was the interference of elected authorities in the free market place and their imposition of restrictions and regulations that were in total disregard of commercial enterprise and activity.

In my last year of employment, my fuel budget was 275 million dollars. I was to administer this expense to the best advantage and when the projections could not be met, it was up to me to provide complete explanations. Management were most understanding of circumstances and when I had to appear before them to see another million or two they were most understanding.

All of the circumstances that were prevalent at the time made me think of the days of my beginning as a telegraph messenger getting a rate of three cents for each message that was delivered. How circumstances can change was beyond my comprehension. I had not so much as graduated from grade ten and now in the business world I was competing with the college graduates, even those who came with university degrees, and here I was sitting behind a desk telling them they were not acceptable as employees due to qualifications. That was the company policy in that degrees and college certifications were of a primary concern, which in my estimation were very false qualifications. I hired people who demonstrated initiative regardless of their scholastic achievements and those people have outlasted me, as I have retired and those of my selection are now still there in their positions carrying on the day-to-day operation.

It is sad to say that in my prime with the years of experience and still of an alert mind, there came a day when I saw people of lesser seniority and lesser age electing to take early retirement. At the time I had some 46 years of service betwixt CP Rail and CP Air and when I saw my cohorts leaving, my first reaction was to seek the same early retirement with the golden handshake being made available to others. That was where I learned that all were not treated equal and while others were getting the salutary release, when I requested the same it was only to find out that they were being put out to pasture and not being replaced. In my case if I were to go out it meant a replacement and since I was not in the dispensable category, I did not qualify for either the early release or the gratuity that was available to those considered as surplus.

There were a number of face to face meetings and in view of my insistence, it was finally agreed that a replacement would be sought and I would be released with a gratuity for the months that were to take for the search. The company in fact hired what are today called "Head Hunters," and while several prospects were proposed, their efforts were mollified by the fact that layoffs were taking place and the company was to be placed into a very embarrassing situation were they now to bring an outsider and new employee into the organization when their own people were being put out onto the street.

Our differences were resolved and with the appointment of Chris Brodkorb as my successor, I was given the option to take my retirement at the end of 1982, having to my credit 46-1/2 years of service with Canadian Pacific (Rail, 1936-1953, and Air, 1953-1982).

Retirement

As I now sit in 1990 and try to put on paper my life experiences, there are many factors that cannot be recalled in the detail that would be justified. Since my exit from the active life as Director of Fuels, I have yet to set foot on another aircraft. The days I spent in those torture chambers going from Europe to Asia or South America with the frequent commutes to Miami, Washington, Dallas, Houston, Ottawa, Montreal, San Francisco or Los Angeles were more than enough to satisfy me for the rest of my life.

Nevertheless, it must be admitted that my final years were perhaps the most satisfying in my career. The Vice President of Finance never questioned any of my actions, I made million dollar purchases over the phone by word of mouth and my decisions were accepted throughout the petroleum industry. Only in isolated long term deals did we have a written agreement. On my signature, funds were advanced in any amount, no questions asked. One or two million was a common request, no approvals from anyone, just my signature. What a far cry from the days of a telegraph messenger when I had to have a recipient's signature to earn three cents!

There were all the fringe benefits that went along with the position — first class on any airline, first class hotels, even a car and chauffeur in some instances where language could be a problem or when schedules were tight. At many airports I was met by our local representatives, maneuvered through back doors and never saw either customs or immigration.

The experiences of the visits to the many countries in my travels can never be replaced by the reading of National Geographic. Be they my visit to Moscow or the viewing of the destitute of the Latin American regions.

The decades of my tenure on this earth have been both rewarding and satisfying. I have enjoyed life to the maximum and been rewarded for my efforts beyond my wildest dreams. How could anyone complain when you have a home, a loving family, a comfortable life cycle where there is no need for denial of one's desires, you're both well fed and warm in the house that is a man's castle with the grass and flowers that make life worth living.

The decades of my devotion to Canadian Pacific have been satisfying in more ways than one. Those of you who read these recollections will probably never understand the evolution that has taken place in my short lifetime on this earth. There was the introduction of synthetic fabrics, the jet aircraft, computers, the local grocery store cash register, the small hand-held calculators or, for that matter, the domestic games and all the other sensory devices that depend on miniscule electrical energy for their operation. We now have the advantages of all the scientific advances, including the television, the microwave, transmission of voice communication and the various technological advances that have been made that are too numerous to mention. Take for an example only one factor and accept what colour television has brought into every household. Just imagine how far this is from the day that we got our first battery operated radio on the farm. Many are the technological advances that could be listed but since that would take another volume, let us accept that the evolution of time has taken technology in stride and those of us here to enjoy the evolution of progress, get to enjoy the benefits that are now at hand.

We are all most fortunate to enjoy the benefits of the advance of technology and I cannot overlook the sacrifices made that are now so beneficial in our society. There were many of my friends and schoolmates who contributed the maximum for the benefit of us that are now enjoying a life in a society of both health and welfare.

My friends made the ultimate contribution.

Leon Poppel, Ted Partington, Eric Cellars

Bob Smith, Harvey Moffatt and Chuck Earl

never came home to enjoy or reap the benefits of their contribution.

The End

Alec at retirement
Beverly Belanger collection

Alec enjoys his retirement with his granddaughters.
Above, working in the yard. Beverly Belanger collection
Below, Marie, Alec, Sylvie and Alicia, Christmas 1995.
Roberta Sonolet collection

More about the Author

Although not mentioned in his memoir, Alec Noble was an active member in the Richmond Rotary Club and served as President 1968-1969.

Alec (Spiridonoff) Noble
Born in Harbin, Manchuria, China
21 September 1919
Died in Vancouver, British Columbia, Canada
21 January 2009, Age: 89

In Loving Memory Of

ALEC NOBLE

September 21, 1919 - January 21, 2009

You are a child of the universe.
No less than the trees & the stars.
You have a right to be here
And whether or not it is clear to you
no doubt the universe is unfolding as it should.
Therefore be at peace with God
whatever you conceive God to be.
And in all your labours & aspirations
in the noisy confusion of life, keep peace
with your soul. With all its sham,
drudgery & broken dreams, it is still
a beautiful world. Be careful,
strive to be happy.

Betty (Haverstock) Noble
Born in Vancouver, British Columbia, Canada
11 October 1926
Died in Vancouver, British Columbia, Canada
5 January 2007, Age: 80

In Loving Memory Of

Betty Marilyn Christine Noble

October 11, 1926 ~ January 5, 2007

Psalm 23

The Lord is my Shepherd; I shall not want.
He maketh me to lie down in green pastures:
He leadeth me beside the still waters.
He restoreth my soul:
He leadeth me in the paths of righteousness
for His name' sake.
Yea, though I walk through
the valley of the shadow of death,
I will fear no evil: For thou art with me;
Thy rod and thy staff, they comfort me.
Thou preparest a table before me
in the presence of mine enemies;
Thou annointest my head with oil;
My cup runneth over.
Surely goodness and mercy shall
follow me all the days of my life,
and I will dwell in the House of the Lord forever.

Appendix A:
A Brief History of Harbin, Manchuria
by Christy Olesen

St. Nicholas Russian Orthodox Church in Harbin, China, 1919
Photo courtesy Stone Lake Area Historical Society, Wisconsin.
Photo by C.M. Winter

When the Russians pushed the Trans Siberian Railway (TSR) east in the late 1890s, they needed to solve two problems when they reached Chita, Russia, near the Siberian and Manchurian border. First, the terrain was rough, and it would be expensive and difficult to build around the swell of Northern China to reach the coast. Second, they coveted rail access to a year-round, frost-free port. To solve both problems they planned to build their railroad across the flat lands of northern Manchuria. (Later, the TSR would build a line north of Manchuria to Vladivostok.) The main line headed east to Vladivostok with a southern line to the year-round Port Author on the Yellow Sea. This main line became the China Eastern Railway (CER), and the southern part became the Southern Manchurian Railway. Both were part of the TSR, now under Chinese ownership, both are major lines of commerce from the coast into China and Russia.

At the beginning of the 20th century, when Alec's father Vasili signed a 25-year contract with the TSR and traveled with the survey team to Manchuria, Harbin was a frontier town comparable to the Old West towns of America. In the following century it became the transportation hub of northeastern China, with a current population exceeding six million, ten million including outlying areas.

In June 1895, the Russian steamship Telegraph steamed west into Manchuria from the Pacific port of Vladivostok on its way to reestablish trade. Expeditions in the previous decades had been met with hostility by the Manchurians. But now there was an increased demand for labor and material needed for the construction of the Ussuri Railroad (a section of the TSR), and Manchuria was the closest source.

Pushing through China presented the Russians many problems. Where the politicians wanted to build a cultural and social bridge to China to encourage trade and commerce, the military saw only more territory to be defended. Where some politicians saw the possibility of new territories to annex, other politicians feared the mingling of races. Treaties were negotiated, and foreign as well as Russian banks were involved.

The plan evolved to find a place to set up a headquarters halfway from the port of Vladivostok - the railway's destination – and the current end of the line in Chita. Russia would then build out in both directions until the railway was complete. The scouting party found a suitable spot in an area known as Khaarbin, on the Sungari River. When the construction crews arrived a few months later, they found the area flooded. They moved a short distance to an area with a bluff above the flood level. There were only a few local resident farmers, and some old distillery ruins. This is where the Russians founded Harbin.

The town grew quickly to accommodate recruits, both Russian and Chinese, brought in to build the railroad. It had to expand again to accommodate the thousands of Russians and tens of thousands of Chinese who poured in looking for work and opportunity on a new frontier. They came despite the area having a reputation as uncivilized and unexplored, with unfavorable climatic conditions, and even bandits. By 1902 there were 15,000 CER employees, 18,000 dependents, and 25,000 in the CER Guard working and living along the entire right-of-way. There were 20,000 residents in Harbin; three quarters of the Russian families worked for CER. The railroad had to provide the necessities of housing, food supplies, medical and sanitary facilities and organize the CER Guard and police, telegraph and postal communications and judicial system,

The first years of settlement experienced anti-foreign incidents including the Boxer Rebellion (1900), which had its origins south of Manchuria. In the Harbin area, the fighting wasn't as fierce and left only one Russian dead and one seriously wounded. The Russo-Japanese War (1904), the first 'great war' of the 20th century, was the result of conflict between Imperial Russia and Imperial Japan over the territories of Manchuria and Korea. Russia needed the year-round, frost-free harbor of Port Arthur for its navy as well as trade. It leased the port from China and wanted Korea as a buffer between Port Arthur and Japan. The Japanese resented the Russian expansion into Asia.

From the time when the first Russian exploration vessel landed in the area, river traffic expanded to more than 5,000 vessels, from over 140 foreign and domestic destinations, docking at Harbin's piers by 1911.

The settlement soon began to morph into a large Eurasian city. By 1915 its nearly 45,000 residents were made up of mostly Russian subjects, making Harbin the largest foreign settlement in China. The 60,000 Chinese, living and working along the railway right-of-way, made Greater Harbin the third-largest "Russian" city east of the Urals. The volume of trade surpassed other regional trade centers.

Representatives of Imperial Russia resided on the bluff in an architectural mix of expensive brick and stone buildings: neoclassical next to art nouveau, sprinkled with whimsical Orientalia. With its busy rail station, Harbin was now acting as Russia's representative to the Far East and was considered a typical provincial Russian city.

Life in Harbin exhibited a certain amount of political freedom and tolerance. Municipal participation and intercultural cooperation were encouraged. When Alec's father Vasili's contract with the TSR ended in 1925, World War 1 (1914) and the Russian Revolution (1917) had already come and gone. Having lived in a politically progressive Russian city, he decided against moving back to communist Russia, now the Soviet Union (Union of Soviet Socialist Republic, 1922–1991). That is when he made the decision to move his family to Canada.

=========

Wolff, David; To the Harbin Station: The Liberal Alternative in Russian Manchuria, 1898-1914. Stanford University Press.

Appendix B:

The Practice of Chinese Foot Binding

by Christy Olesen

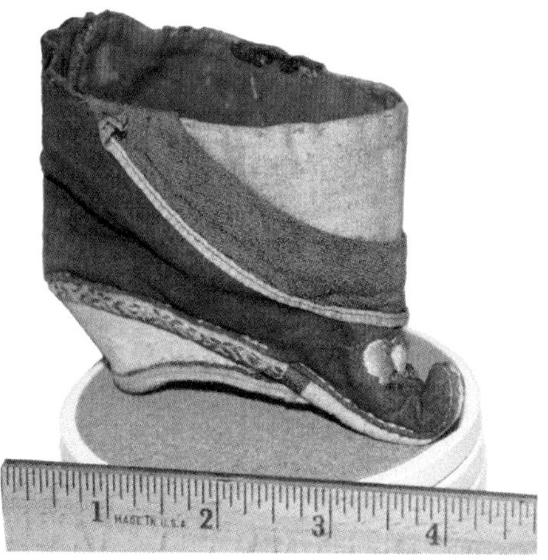

Hand stitched shoe worn by a woman with bound feet in China, c. 1880, from the family collection of Christy Olesen. Photo by Christy Olesen

The origin of foot binding in China is not clear. There are several possibilities: One story tells of the concubine Daii, in the Shang Dynasty (aprox. 1766-1046 B.C.), who had clubfeet and wanted all girls' feet bound so her feet would be the standard of beauty. Another story tells of the courtesan of Emperor Xiao Baojuan (483-501 A.D.), Pan Yu'er. She had delicate feet, and when she danced, the emperor expressed admiration for her small feet. The most likely is that foot binding originated in the time of Emperor Li Yu (Southern Tang Dynasty 937-976 A.D.). The emperor asked his concubine, Yao Niang, to bind her feet with white silk and to dance a lotus dance on her toes. She was graceful and seemed to skim on top of the 'golden lotus.' After this, other upperclass women began to bind their feet.

Bound feet were considered a mark of beauty and privilege.

Tiny feet were considered feminine and dainty. Delicate feet were considered a prerequisite for marriage. Eldest daughters of the lower classes had their feet bound from a young age so that they could marry into the upper classes. Their younger sister were destined to work as bondservants, domestic slaves or alongside their working husbands and did not have their feet bound.

Walking on bound feet could only be done by bending the knees and swaying back and forth to swing the foot forward. It was considered erotic to men. Many women led lives of debility, depending on servants or family to do for them what they could not do for themselves.
The severest form of foot binding was very painful for the young women subjected to it. Started around age seven, the arch of the foot and the toes were broken. The foot was bent and the smaller toes were curled under with only the big toe in its original position. This gave the small, delicate, pointed-toe shape the men found so alluring. A size of three inches was considered the ideal size.

In some parts of China, foot binding was less drastic. The feet were bound to keep them small and narrow but no bones were broken. In other parts of the country it was not practiced at all.

In 1644, Manchu women were forbidden to bind their feet by an edict from the emperor. However, few complied. Woman's Christian Temperance Movement argued for discontinuation in 1883. Missionaries advocated the movement to quit the practice as a way to help foster equality between the sexes. Soon educated Chinese could see that foot binding did not reflect their progress in a modern world. Imperial edicts in 1902 outlawed the practice, but it wasn't until the Communists took power in 1949 that the laws were enforced.

Appendix C:
The Significance of the Queue
by Christy Olesen

Chinese market street, c. 1885, from the family collection of Christy Olesen. Photo by Albert Huntley

A queue is the long braid worn for centuries by men in China, primarily by the Manchu of Manchuria. The head was shaved above the temples and the rest of the hair gathered at the back and braided. The braid was mandatory. It was considered treason to not wear the hairstyle, and treason was punishable by death.

Once in power, Nurhaci (1559-1626), who defeated the Ming Dynasty and created the Aisin Gioro Dynasty (1616-1626), mandated that all Hun men in the conquered areas adopt the queue hairstyle. It made it easy to identify the rebels who refused to accept Qing rule and the queue.
The history of the queue is a bloody one filled with conquest, rebellion and executions.

Queues are also known in Native American cultures. British soldiers and sailors of the 18th century wore a similar hairstyle called a queue. Though usually not braided, the hair was pulled tightly to the back. A queue was mandatory in the Prussian Army until 1807.

Early in the 20th century, after the fall of the Qing Dynasty, adherence to the queue in northern China was discontinued. After 1920, when the Emperor of China Puyi cut his queue, most men abandoned the custom.

Appendix D:
A Brief History of Canadian Pacific Railway

By Carol Morse

Canadian Pacific Rail c. 1920s. Wikimedia Commons

The Canadian Pacific Railway (CPR), built during 1881 through 1885, is a story of achieving an impossible dream. Visionaries saw the railway as a way to develop the sparsely populated Prairie Provinces. They wanted a cross-country railroad that stretched from Ontario and Quebec to British Colombia. They persevered, overcoming severe obstacles. The company faced challenges such as building a railway through the Canadian Rockies and making way through some difficult terrain in Northern Ontario. In Alberta, Chief Blackfoot was given lifetime privileges to travel on the train in exchange for allowing the railroad to cross his land.

CPR chose a southerly route closer to the American border, which prevented American railways from intruding on the

Canadian railway market. Major Rogers, a surveyor, found a needed pass in the Selkirk Mountains in British Colombia in 1881. CPR gave him $5,000 and named it "Rogers Pass." Kicking Horse Pass on the Alberta-British Colombia border, a very high summit (5,331 ft. with a steep drop to 1,150 ft.), presented another challenge. CPR had to take expensive measures to assure safety. Years later, spiral tunnels built in the 20th century solved the problem. Generally, European immigrants and Chinese coolies worked on the railway. On November 7, 1885, Director Smith drove the last stake for the railway in a special ceremony at Craigellachie, British Colombia.

Seven months later, the railway was ready for operation. The first transcontinental passenger train left Montreal at 8 p.m., June 28, 1886 and arrived at Port Moody, British Colombia July 4, 1886. (Later, Granville, renamed Vancouver, replaced Port Moody as Terminal.) This first train had two baggage cars, a mail car, one second-class coach, two immigrant sleepers, two first-class coaches, two sleeping cars and a diner.

In 1881 CPR was given the right to create and charge for both electric telegraph and telephone services. In cities, telegraph boys were messengers. They rode bicycles to deliver messages and pick up the replies. Sometimes messages were telephoned ahead. By 1931, it became the Communications Department, as telephone lines, news wire, etc. were implemented. This was Alec's first job at CPR.

In 1889 CPR leased the New Brunswick railway for 99 years and built the International Railway of Maine, which connected Montreal with Saint John, New Brunswick, making it the first transcontinental railway company in Canada. This railway gave access year-round for trans-Atlantic cargo and passenger service. Because of sea ice, the Gulf of St. Lawrence closed the Port of Montreal during the winter.

Few people lived in the prairies when the railway began operation. In order to prosper, CPR needed passengers and cargo. In the original contract, the government had granted CPR 25 million acres for the railway. To promote immigration, the company began selling some of that land by advertising in European newspapers and in eastern Canada. Hearing about the fertile farmland in the Canadian prairies, immigrants responded. In 1884, experimental farms were set up along the tracks. In 1909 CPR spent more on promoting immigration than the Canadian government.

CPR sold ready-made farms with house, barn, well and pump to facilitate settlers in adapting to the new environment. Imagine getting a 65-130 hectare farm already fenced with one-third part plowed and ready for planting. From Wetaskwin, Alberta to Saskatoon, Sask., there were 762 such farms available at the dream price of ten annual payments of $1,300 for smaller farms and ten $2,500 annual payments for larger farms.

In the years 1901 to 1928, CPR continued to expand and improve its operations. In November, 1909, the Lethbridge Viaduct over the Oldman River Valley at Lethbridge, Alberta opened. It measured 5,328 ft. long and at maximum, 315 ft. high, notably one of the longest railway bridges in Canada at that time. In 1916, CPR replaced Rogers pass with the five-mile long Connaught Tunnel under Mount Macdonald. At the time, this was the longest railway tunnel in the Western Hemisphere. At the same time, CPR was building hotels in strategic locations.

During World War I, CPR contributed greatly to the war effort, providing not only rail transport but also ships, shops, hotels, telegraphs and personnel.

Until the 1960s, passenger trains served as the primary mode of transportation for long distance travel. New immigrants going to the Prairie Provinces, soldiers, particularly in wartime, and upper class tourists rode the trains. The company also had "boat trains," linking a train to a port with boat passage to yet another train. This service was discontinued in 1965.

The company's services down through the years also included special trains. From the 1890s to 1933, CPR moved raw silk from Vancouver, having been shipped from the Orient, to silk mills in New York and New Jersey. One train might carry silk valued at several million dollars. Silk trains phased out when nylon was invented at the end of World War II. CPR also had a funeral train, to carry the remains of a famous person such as Sir William Cornelius Van Horne, former CPR president on Sept. 14, 1915.

In 1939, King George VI and Queen Elizabeth came to visit Canada, taking them on a rail tour. CPR took them from Quebec to Vancouver.

The steam locomotive was "the engine that could." From 1906 to 1948, the locomotives progressively had greater capabilities. In fact, CPR built hundreds of locomotives in its Montreal shops. The largest locomotive, the Selkirk built in 1929, could handle steep grades. After 1949, CPR generally used diesel locomotives.

Today, CPR has a different face. The Canadian Pacific Railway Limited, formed in 2001, is a Canadian rail transportation company that operates Canadian Pacific Railway.

Indeed, CPR was a dream realized that brought prosperity to Canada.

=========

Canadian Pacific Railway. Wikipedia.
Canadian Pacific Railway. www.cpr.ca/en/about-cp/our-past.

Appendix E:
A Brief History of Canadian Pacific Airline
By Carol Morse

CP Air Douglas DC-8-55CF-Jet at London Gatwick Airport 1977.
From the Eduard Marmet collection - Wikimedia Commons.

The metamorphosis of the Canadian Pacific Airlines (CPA) was like a caterpillar in a cocoon. From its humble beginnings, the company had a fleet consisting of ten bush airlines purchased in the early 1940s along with Canadian Airways in 1942.

Struggling in the cocoon stage, CPA contended with the government-owned Trans-Canada Airlines (TCA).

Pacific Airlines was a chief rival of TCA. As a government owned company, TCA made sure it had a monopoly on routes. The federal government placed limits on "domestic market share" restricting routes like Vancouver to Toronto or

Toronto to New York. International agreements restricted CPA from routes to destinations like London or Paris.

Despite the obstacles, CPA, in addition to domestic cross-country flights, developed five key overseas routes to destinations such as Amsterdam, Australia and Hong Kong. Vancouver served as CPA's base. The company started with DC4 and later DC6 aircraft. By 1961, CPR was using Douglas DC8 jetliners.

Indeed the butterfly was emerging from the cocoon as the Airline grew. In 1968 the company became known as CP AIR to concur with other Canadian Pacific Railway subsidiaries. It was also the first airline to have a nonstop flight between North America and mainline China in 1987.

When the government lifted its restrictions on trans-continental flights in 1979, CP AIR had to immediately upgrade its fleet in order to use the newly available routes. This would cost the company one billion dollars.

By 1980 the butterfly was floundering. In addition to massive debt, CP Air had greater competition and Asia was suffering from economic downturn. In 1986 the company once again became Canadian Pacific Airline. However, this was short-lived for in 1987, CPA sold along with Quebec's Nordair for $300 million. The buyer, Pacific Western Airlines (Calgary based) assumed the debt. The airline would become Canadian Airline International until it merged with Air Canada in 2000.

==========
Canadian Airways. en.wikipedia.org/wiki/Canadian_Airways
Trans-Canada Airline. www.thecanadianencyclopedia.ca
Canadian Pacific Airlines. Wikipedia.

Acknowledgments

Thanks to Beverly Belanger and Roberta Sonolet for their enthusiastic support in publishing their father's memoir and contributing most of the photos.

Thanks to Delyna Kitsman for her excellent transcription of Alec's handwritten manuscript. Luckily, Alec had beautiful handwriting. And for being my editor's editor.

Thanks to Margaret Olesen for diligently tracking down Beverly and Roberta when I found that I had out-of-date contact information.

About The Editor

Christy Olesen has always been fascinated with family history and genealogy but never had as much time as she wished to pursue the study beyond collecting family oral history. When she read Alec's memoir, she recognized it as a story that needed to be published. She felt the poor-immigrant, high-school-dropout-makes-good story would have a wide appeal. Related to Alec by marriage through her mother's cousin, Christy counts his story a rich addition to her extended family's history.

Christy writes clean/sweet, small town romance and founded Indie-Pendent Publishing Company. She's an accomplished graphic artist and an award winning watercolor artist. She lives among extended family at the base of the Sierra Nevada.

***

Carol Morse writes and illustrates children's stories. She is also an editor and copywriter. Carol has an MA in English with a TESOL (Teaching English to Speakers of Other Languages) emphasis and served as an adjunct professor in several community colleges in southern California. She lives in Carson Valley, Nevada.

About The Publisher

Indie-Pendent Publishing Company was started to facilitate the publication of the founder's novels and her family's history through memoirs of interest to a wide audience.

www.indie-pendentpublishing.com

The IPPC book list includes:

STORY OF AN IMMIGRANT: a Russian boy born in China prospers in Canada, by Alec (Spiridonoff) Noble 2014

A DADDY FOR LUKE by Christy Olesen 2013

HER SCOTTISH CEO by Christy Olesen 2012

Coming soon:

THE JOHN MUIR TRAIL: one family, one month, 250 miles by Margaret Olesen with additional material by John (Jackie) Olesen

Available through www.indie-pendentpublishing.com

Indie-Pendent Publishing Co.

Published by Indie-Pendent Publishing Company

Edited by Christy Olesen
Additional historical material by Carol Morse
Cover design Copyright © 2014 by Christy Olesen
Cover images:

Alec Noble – Beverly Belanger collection.
Alberta Prairies – Thinkstock.
CP Air DC-8-63 Toronto 1977 - clipperartic/Wikimedia Commons.

Indie-Pendent Publishing Co.
www.indie-pendentpublishing.com

Made in the USA
Charleston, SC
17 April 2016